About this book

Symbols are used to denote the following categories:

🞥 map reference to maps on cover
✉ address or location
☎ telephone number
🕐 opening times
💷 admission charge
🍴 restaurant or café on premises
   or nearby
🚇 nearest underground train station

🚌 nearest bus/tram route
🚉 nearest overground train station
⛴ nearest ferry stop
✈ nearest airport
❓ other practical information
ℹ tourist information office
► indicates the page where you will
   find a fuller description

This book is divided into five sections.

The essence of Austria pages 6–19
Introduction; Features; Food and drink;
Short break including the 10 Essentials

Planning pages 20–33
Before you go; Getting there; Getting
around; Being there

Best places to see pages 34–55
The unmissable highlights of any visit
to Austria

Best things to do pages 56–79
Good places to have lunch; places to
take the children; best souvenir shops;
top scenic routes; opera and classical
music and more

Exploring pages 80–186
The best places to visit in Austria,
organized by area

Maps
All map references are to the maps on
the covers. For example, Kitzbühel has
the reference 🞥 2E – indicating the grid
square in which it is to be found.

Admission prices
Inexpensive (under €6)
Moderate (€6–€12)
Expensive (over €12)

Hotel prices
Price are per ~

D1428293

... meal per person
without drinks:
€ budget (under €12);
€€ moderate (€12–€22);
€€€ expensive (over €22)

Contents

BEST THINGS TO DO

EXPLORING...

The essence of...

Though no longer the centre of a multinational empire, Austria retains strong regional diversity. Hungarian and Croat influences in the east, Slovenian and Italian in the south, Swiss in the west, and German in the northwest mean that, even today, there's not one but many Austrias at the heart of Europe. Vienna apart, the culture is predominantly rural, with the emphasis on traditional values and customs. Austria is a deeply conservative country and its people, especially in the rural Catholic areas, are remarkably devout (10 of the national holidays are religious in origin). As a people, Austrians are friendly and courteous, and everywhere you go you'll be assured of a warm welcome.

THE ESSENCE OF AUSTRIA

features

Think of Austria and inevitably it is scenery that springs to mind: the view from the train window as you cross the Semmering Pass, the cable-car ascent of the Pfänder overlooking Bodensee (Lake Constance), the ferry across the lake to Hallstatt or the exhilarating drive on the Grossglockner mountain highway. No wonder the Austrian landscapes have inspired so many composers from Haydn, Mozart and Beethoven to Bruckner, Schubert and Strauss. Salzburg is the birthplace of Mozart and the venue of the annual Salzburg Festival. There are dozens of other musical celebrations up and down the country and some extraordinary locations – the most spectacular being the floating stage at Bregenz, where the Bodensee provides the backdrop.

GEOGRAPHY

● Austria lies at the heart of central Europe. It shares borders with Switzerland, Germany, the Czech Republic, Slovakia, Hungary, Slovenia, Italy and Liechtenstein. It is one of the most heavily wooded countries in Europe – 46 per cent of the terrain is forested. The Tirol (west) is the most mountainous region – the highest peak is Grossglockner (3,797m/12,457ft).

WINTER SPORTS

- Nearly 50 per cent of the population goes alpine skiing, cross-country skiing or snowboarding regularly.

Austria has:

- More than 3,500 ski lifts
- 23,000km (14,300 miles) of downhill ski trails
- 12,400 skiing instructors in 900 resorts
- 1,300 artificial skating rinks

THE PEOPLE

- More than 98 per cent of Austria's population of 8,200,000 is German speaking, although there are small minorities of Croats, Hungarians, Slovenes, Czechs, Slovaks and Romany peoples. In a predominantly rural country, Vienna is the only city with a population in excess of one million.

NATIONAL PARKS

There are six national parks, see: www.national parksaustria.at.

- **Nationalpark Donau-Auen:** the largest single wetland in central Europe, home to more than 5,000 animal species.
- **Nationalpark Gesäuse:** a region of diverse habitats in northern Styria covering 11,000ha (27,180 acres) of mountains, forest, alpine meadows and stretches of water.
- **Nationalpark Hohe Tauern (► 42–43):** a vast Alpine nature reserve in three provinces (eastern Tirol, Carinthia and Salzburg).
- **Nationalpark Kalkalpen:** in the Pyhrn-Eisenwurzen region, a typical high-Alpine park.
- **Nationalpark Neusiedler See-Seewinkel (► 124–125):** the only steppe reserve in central Europe, best visited in spring and autumn.
- **Nationalpark Thayatal:** meadowland on the border with the Czech Republic.

food & drink

Austrians love their food but with the emphasis on *bürgerliche Küche* – loosely translated as nourishing, hearty fare – rather than haute cuisine. Meat is the staple of the traditional diet, cooked in rich cream or wine sauces and served up with generous helpings of potatoes, dumplings and sauerkraut (pickled cabbage). However, healthier, more sensible eating is catching on, especially among the young, and nowadays most kitchens place greater emphasis on quality over quantity.

Austria's imperial past and its location at the heart of Europe account for the surprising diversity of the national cuisine. In Burgenland for example, *Gulash* (paprika-flavoured beef stew), and *Letscho* (stewed tomatoes mixed with spices and green pepper) are reminders that until the 1920s this region belonged to Hungary. Further south in Styria, Balkan influences make themselves felt in dishes such as

Bohnensuppe, a spicy bean soup, and *Cevapcici* (meatballs cooked in a piquant tomato sauce). Styria's homegrown specialities include *Steirisches Wurzelfleisch* (pork cooked with root vegetables), and you should certainly try *Kürbiskernöl* (pumpkin seed oil) on salads. Dumplings originated in Bohemia and Upper Austria is still sometimes referred to as 'dumpling land'. Look especially for *Semmel-knödel*, small pieces of bread soaked in milk and mixed with flour, egg, herbs and spices. A Tirolean variant, *Nockerl*, is made with a white cheese dough and flavoured with bacon or spinach. The 'national' dish of the Tirol is *Gröstel*, a delicious pan-fried offering prepared with sliced potatoes, pork, onions and spices. In Vienna you can try all of these dishes, not forgetting of course *Wienerschnitzel*

(veal or pork cutlet fried in breadcrumbs). The quintessential Viennese dish is *Tafelspitz*, boiled fillet of beef served with potatoes and horseradish sauce – a favourite with the Emperor Franz-Josef.

WINE

Austria is a major producer of excellent wines. *Veltliner*, made from the Grüner Veltliner grape, is the country's best known white wine. Dry, fragrant and a touch spicy, it's best encountered in a *Heuriger* (wine tavern). *Welschriesling* is fruitier, though decidedly inferior to *Rheinriesling*, produced in the Wachau. The best known red wine is *Blaufränkisch* – dry and highly palatable; it goes very well with meat dishes. *Zweigelt*, also dry, has a bit more body. Even better is the muscat-flavoured *St Laurent* or, if you happen to be in Burgenland, *Esterházy*, a superb wine still produced on the Eisenstadt estate.

DESSERTS

Forget watching your waistline and throw caution to the winds – Austrian desserts are an art form. *Apfelstrudel* (apples and raisins, wrapped in pastry and sprinkled with sugar) goes down

well, as does *Sachertorte*, a wickedly rich chocolate cake with a layer of apricot jam under its chocolate icing. Other popular desserts include *Topfentorte* (cheesecake), *Palatschinken* (pancakes, usually with fruit or jam fillings), *Mohr im Hemd* ('Moor in a shirt', a chocolate pudding with sauce and whipped cream) or – Mozart's favourite – *Salzburger Nockerln*, a sweet egg soufflé flavoured with vanilla and sugar.

THE ESSENCE OF AUSTRIA

short break

If you have only a short time to visit Austria and would like to take home some unforgettable memories, you can do something local and capture the real flavour of the country. The following suggestions will give you a wide range of sights and experiences that won't take very long, won't cost very much and will make your visit very special.

● **Visit a traditional coffee house** Read the morning paper over a coffee and pastry.

● **Breathe the mountain air** Whatever the season, head for the mountains.

● **Visit a *Heuriger*** These vineyard taverns on the outskirts of Vienna are for sampling the new wines while listening to folksy music in relaxed garden surroundings.

● **Go to a concert** Austria is renowned as a land of music – at least nine famous composers were either born or made their home here.

● **Stroll through old Vienna** Admire the stately architecture of the Graben on your way to Stephansdom (St Stephen's Cathedral).

● **Pay homage to Mozart** Visit Mozart's birthplace and apartment in Salzburg.

● **Take a boat trip** Austria is blessed with countless beautiful lakes – Wörther See, Neusiedler See and Hallstätter See, to name but three.

● **Visit a mine** Something of an Austrian speciality, the workings of the salt and silver mines which made the country prosperous are now among its top tourist attractions.

● **Try some regional cooking** Wherever you're staying in Austria, there'll be at least one local dish to savour. There can be few more satisfying ways to learn about a country's traditions.

● **Explore the Wienerwald (Vienna Woods)** One of central Europe's most famous green spaces can be enjoyed on foot, on horseback, in a car or by bicycle.

Planning

Before you go

WHEN TO GO

JAN	FEB	MAR	APR	MAY	JUN	JUL	AUG	SEP	OCT	NOV	DEC
1°C	3°C	9°C	15°C	19°C	23°C	26°C	25°C	20°C	15°C	7°C	4°C
34°F	37°F	48°F	59°F	66°F	73°F	79°F	77°F	68°F	59°F	45°F	39°F

◖ High season   ◖ Low season

Austria has a temperate Central European climate, which is greatly affected by the Alps. Summers are generally warm, with cool nights, though Vienna and other low-lying cities and towns can get uncomfortably hot during July and August.

Winters are cold, below freezing in January and February. Snow levels are usually high enough for winter sports across the country. The ski season in the Alps runs from December to April, while in summer the mountains are particularly popular with walkers and climbers.

The warm, dry wind called the *Föhn* can also affect the tempertaure, particularly in autumn and spring, when it can melt snow quickly, causing avalanches.

WHAT YOU NEED

● Required
○ Suggested
▲ Not required

Some countries require a passport to remain valid for a minimum period (usually at least six months) beyond the date of entry – contact their consulate or embassy or your travel agent for details.

	UK	Germany	USA	Netherlands	Spain
Passport (or National Identity Card where applicable)	●	●	●	●	▲
Visa (regulations can change – check before you travel)	▲	▲	▲	▲	▲
Onward or Return Ticket	▲	▲	▲	▲	▲
Health Inoculations (tetanus and polio)	▲	▲	▲	▲	▲
Health Documentation (► 23, Health Insurance)	○	○	○	○	○
Travel Insurance	○	○	○	○	○
Driving Licence (national)	●	●	●	●	●
Car Insurance Certificate	●	●	●	●	●
Car Registration Document	●	●	●	●	●

WEBSITES

www.aboutaustria.org
www.alltravelaustria.com
www.austria.info

www.austria-tourism.at
www.aua.com
www.wien.info

TOURIST OFFICES AT HOME

In the UK

The tourist office in London is for press and marketing purposes only, however, you can make enquiries by phone (tel: 0845 101 1818) and get through direct to Austria (local UK call charges apply). Alternatively email holiday@austria.info

In the USA

The same applies in New York as in London. Tel: 212/944-6880 (answering service). Alternatively email travel@austria.info

HEALTH INSURANCE

Insurance Citizens of the EU can receive free hospital treatment on production of the relevant documentation (EHIC – European Health Insurance Card), but private medical insurance is still advised and is essential for all other travellers. Visitors from the US and Canada should check their insurance coverage.

Dental services If you require urgent treatment, there is an emergency dental helpline in Vienna: Emergency Dentist tel: 5122078.

TIME DIFFERENCES

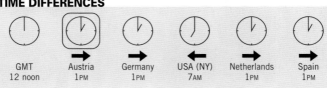

GMT	Austria	Germany	USA (NY)	Netherlands	Spain
12 noon	1PM	1PM	7AM	1PM	1PM

Austria is on Central European Time, one hour ahead of Greenwich Mean Time (GMT+1), 6 hours ahead of New York and 9 hours behind Sydney.

NATIONAL HOLIDAYS

1 January *New Year's Day*

6 January *Epiphany*

March/April *Easter Monday*

1 May *Labour Day*

6th Thu after Easter *Ascension Day*

6th Mon after Easter *Whit Monday*

June (date varies) *Corpus Christi*

15 August *Assumption Day*

26 October *National Day*

1 November *All Saints' Day*

8 December *Immaculate Conception*

25 December *Christmas Day*

26 December *St Stephen's Day*

Most shops, offices and museums close on these days.

WHAT'S ON WHEN

January *New Year's Day Concert:* performed by the Vienna Philharmonic Orchestra in the Musikverein.

Mozartwoche (Mozart Week): one of Salzburg's many celebrations of the great composer's music.

February *Fasching* (Carnival): culminates in the Shrove Tuesday festivities all over the country.

Opernball: Vienna Opera Ball.

March to mid-May *Bregenz Spring Festival:* music and dance.

Mid-May to June *Wiener Festwochen* (Vienna Festival): opera, music, theatre and film.

Mid-May to late October Concerts of music by Haydn in Schloss Esterházy, Eisenstadt, culminating in the *International Haydn Festival.*

June *Corpus Christi:* in the Salzkammergut towns of Ebensee, Traunsee and Hallstatt, with flower-bedecked barge processions on the lakes. *Danube Island Festival:* mega-party which in the past has attracted internationally known bands.

Mid-June to mid-July *Styriarte:* the Graz festival of classical music under Nikolaus Harnoncourt.

July to mid-September *Klangbogen Wien:* Vienna's Music Festival of grand opera, chamber music, orchestral concerts. Includes two weeks of jazz in July.

July–August Music concerts in Schloss Ambras, Innsbruck, culminating in the *Festival of Old Music.*
Bad Ischl: operetta weeks.
Open-air Operetta Festival: in Mörbisch, Neusiedler See.
International Musikwoche: Millstatt's chamber music festival.
Bregenz Festival: classical opera on a floating stage on the Bodensee (Lake Constance).
Salzburg International Festival: of opera and music.

September–October *The International Bruckner Festival:* in Linz, opening with fireworks and including theatre and art exhibitions as well as concerts.
Styrian Autumn Festival: in Graz introduces avant-garde music, film, art and theatre.

Late October *'Viennale'* film festival: including experimental films.
Wien Modern: a festival of contemporary classical music.

November *Salzburger Jazz Herbst:* international and local groups.

December *Christkindlmärkte (Christmas markets):* held in the cities. Innsbruck marks St Nicholas' Day (6 Dec) with a procession.
On Christmas Eve, the places to be are the chapel at Oberndorf, near Salzburg, which holds a service that includes the singing of *Silent Night*, composed by local organist, Franz Gruber; and St Stephen's Cathedral, Vienna, where midnight Mass is a social event – you'll need to get an entrance pass in advance.

Getting there

BY AIR

Vienna

15km (9 miles) to city centre

🚆 25 minutes

🚌 25 minutes

🚗 25 minutes

Salzburg (west)

12.5km (7.5 miles) to city centre

🚆 15 minutes

🚌 15 minutes

🚗 15 minutes

The major international airport is Vienna (VIE), about 15km (9 miles) southeast of the city centre, but due to the increase in low-cost airlines in Europe, Salzburg, Graz, Klagenfurt, Linz and Innsbruck also take international flights. The national carrier is the Austrian Airlines Group (www.aua.com).

BY RAIL

Trains from the west (Germany and Switzerland) arrive in Vienna at Westbahnhof, trains from the south (Italy and Slovenia) arrive at Südbahnhof. Regional trains to northern Austria leave from Franz-Josefs-Bahnhof. For further information try www.oebb.at.

BY CAR

The A1 Westautobahn links Vienna with Salzburg and Linz in the west, the A2 Südautobahn links Vienna with Klagenfurt and Graz in the south.

DRIVING

- Driving is on the right.
- Speed limit on motorways: 130kph (80mph). A toll is payable – cars must display a sticker (Pickerl) before using the motorway.
  Speed limit on trunk roads: 100kph (62mph).
  Speed limit on urban roads: 50kph (31mph); in some towns special 20kph (12.5mph) limits apply.
- Seatbelts, back and front, are compulsory. Children under 12 may not ride in the front.
- Random breath testing takes place. Never drive under the influence of alcohol; penalties are severe.
- Dipped headlights must be switched on when driving, day and night.
- All petrol is unleaded – 91-octane regular, 95-octane super and diesel. Prices are uniform throughout the country and some petrol stations close on Sundays in rural areas.
- The Österreichischer Automobile, Motorrad und Touring Club (ÖAMTC) tel: 120 and the Auto-, Motor- und Radfahrerbund Österreichs (ARBÖ) tel: 123, both operate callout services for breakdowns and accept AA and RAC insurance coverage. High-visibility vests must be worn if walking on the motorway or if you break down.

Getting around

PUBLIC TRANSPORT

Internal flights Internal flights are operated by the Austrian Airlines Group – Tyrolean Airways.

Rail Austrian Federal Railways – Österreichische Bundesbahnen (ÖBB) – runs efficient, comfortable services throughout the country, covering the main towns and many remarkably scenic routes, and are a great way to see the country. Some long-distance trains have women-only compartments and children's playpens (check the timetables for details).

Austria also has cogwheel railways and many narrow-gauge tracks – a few offering steam train excursions during the summer. For more information contact ÖBB, Bahn-Totalservice, Wien Westbahnhof ☎ 05 1717.

Trams/buses Austria has a good network of bus and coach services, which are cheaper than trains and cover outlying areas, but of course take longer. Vienna, Graz and Innsbruck have trams as well as buses.

Metro Vienna has a fast and efficient 5-line U-Bahn and rapid transit commuter trains (S-Bahn) which connect the suburbs and the airport.

Boats Danube boats carry passengers between Passau, Vienna and Budapest (Apr–Oct). ÖBB operates routes on the Danube and ferries on

the Bodensee (Lake Constance) and Wolfgangsee, while private companies ferry passengers on the other lakes.

CAR RENTAL

Renting cars in Austria is quite expensive and it's usually cheaper to make reservations from home. Major car rental companies have branches in most towns and at airports. An Austrian agency is: Buchbinder ✉ Schlachthausgasse 38, Vienna ☎ 01 717 50 966.

TAXIS

Fares are metred and taxis are not unreasonably expensive. In Vienna, expect to pay surcharges for luggage, for Sundays and bank holidays, for trips to the airport and after 11pm.

FARES AND TICKETS

There are few concessions for foreign visitors on public transport, but if you are making several journeys in a 24-hour period around a city, day tickets almost always represent excellent value.

Museums and galleries normally offer some reductions on the entry price for holders of an International Student Identity Card (ISIC), but for those over retirement age, locally issued ID is usually required to qualify for a reduced-rate ticket. It is still worth asking, so make sure you carry some ID with you, such as a passport or a driver's licence.

ÖBB offer a Seniorenpass for discounted rail travel (you will need a photograph and identification). When renting a car, ask for promotional discounts, sometimes available to senior citizens.

Being there

TOURIST OFFICES
Every town and village has its own tourist office, which provides maps and brochures. Some will book accommodation for you, others will direct you to a hotel booking agent.

Head Office
Austrian National Tourist Office
www.austria-tourism.at

Regional Offices
● Vienna ✉ Obere Augartenstrasse 40, A-1025 Wien ☎ 01 24 555; www.wien.info
● Carinthia (Kärnten) ✉ Casinoplatz 1, A-9220 Velden ☎ 0463 3000; www.kaernten.at

● Salzburger Land ✉ Wiener Bundestrasse 23, Hallwang bei Salzburg, A-5300 Salzburg ☎ 0662 66880; www.salzburgerland.com
● Styria (Steiermark) ✉ St Peter Hauptstrasse 243, A-8042 Graz ☎ 0316 4003-0; www.steiermark.com
● Tirol ✉ Maria-Theresienstrasse 55, A-6010 Innsbruck ☎ 0512 72720; www.tirol.at
● Vorarlberg ✉ Bahnhofstrasse 14/4, Postfach 302, A-6901 Bregenz ☎ 05574 425250; www.vorarlberg-tourism.at

MONEY
The Austrian unit of currency is the euro (€). Euro notes are issued in denominations of 5, 10, 20, 50, 100, 200 and 500 euros. Coins are issued in denominations of 1 and 2 euros and 1, 2, 5, 20 and 50 cents.
Credit cards (Visa, MasterCard, Amex and Diner's Club) are accepted by the larger hotels, restaurants and some garages but smaller establishments prefer cash. ATMs for cash advances can be found outside banks in all tourist areas and major towns.

TIPS/GRATUITIES

Yes ✓ No ✗		
Restaurants (round up bill)	✓	10%
Cafés (round up bill)	✓	50c–€5
Taxis	✓	10%
Porters	✓	€1
Tour guides	✓	€2
Cloakroom attendants	✓	€1
Toilets	✓	50c

POSTAL AND INTERNET SERVICES

Post Office *(Postamt)* opening times are generally Mon–Fri 8–12, 2–6. In major cities hours extend through lunchtime and into Saturday morning and at least one office will be open 24 hours. Stamps are sold at post offices and tobacco kiosks *(tabak-trafik)*. Post boxes are yellow.

Large cities and some smaller towns have internet cafés with a charge of around 2–3 euros per hour. Most large airports and some railway stations provide WiFi and many mid-range and upmarket hotels have internet access as standard.

TELEPHONES

Austrian phone booths are generally dark green with yellow roofs. All boxes, even the new glass ones, display the symbol of a post horn. Most boxes will only accept phone cards which are sold by post offices and tobacconists. You may see local numbers followed by a hyphen and a couple of extra digits – this is the extension and can be called direct.

Emergency telephone numbers
Police 133

Ambulance 144

Fire 122

International dialling codes
From Austria to:
UK: 00 44
Germany: 00 49
USA and Canada: 00 1
Netherlands: 00 31

France: 00 33
International operator: 0900 118 877
Directory enquiries: 118 877

EMBASSIES AND CONSULATES

USA ☎ 01 31339
UK ☎ 01 716 130
Germany ☎ 01 71154

Netherlands ☎ 01 589 39
Spain ☎ 01 505 5788

ELECTRICITY
Electric current is 220 volts AC and appliances need two-round-pin
continental plugs.

HEALTH AND SAFETY
Sun advice The sun is not a real problem in Austria. Take the usual
precautions, especially during the sunniest months (June, July and
August) and when on the ski slopes.

Drugs Pharmacies *(Apotheken)* are the only places that sell over-the-
counter medicines. Take all prescription medicines with you.

Personal safety Austria is among the safest countries in Europe from the
traveller's point of view, but it's sensible to take the usual precautions,
especially on public transport.

● Watch your bag in tourist areas.
● Never leave anything of value visible in your car.
● Deposit your valuables in the hotel safe.
● Avoid walking alone at night.

OPENING HOURS

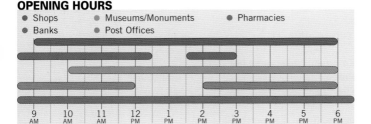

Many shops take a 1- to 2-hour lunch break and open Saturday 8–1. In
Vienna banks stay open until 5:30 on Thursdays. Museums open Sat–Sun
9–6, and 9–4 in winter. Many museums in Vienna and Salzburg close
Mondays, other days in other places. Check in advance with the tourist
office. Pharmacies operate a rota system to provide a 24-hour service –
details are posted on the shop doors. On national holidays banks, offices
and most shops close. However, restaurants, museums and other tourist
attractions tend to stay open, some with restricted hours.

LANGUAGE

Austria's official language is German. A quick pronunciation guide: ä is pronounced like English air, ö like err, ü like oo; au is ow (as in now), oo is or; ie is always ee and ei always eye. The character 'ß' (eg in Straße) is equivalent to 'ss'. All nouns are capitalized.

yes/no	*ja/nein*	today	*heute*
please/thank you	*bitte/danke*	excuse me please	*Entschuldigen*
hello	*Guten Tag/Grüss*		*Sie bitte*
	Gott	yesterday/tomorrow	*gestern/morgen*
goodbye	*Auf Wiedersehen*	where is?	*wo ist?*
good morning	*Guten Morgen*	here	*hier*
good evening	*Guten Abend*	how are you?	*wie geht es Ihnen?*
money	*das Geld*	free (no charge)	*gratis/umsonst*
bank	*die Bank*	more/less	*mehr/weniger*
post office	*das Postamt*	large/small	*gross/klein*
credit card	*Kreditkarte*	the bill	*die Rechnung*
cheap/expensive	*billig/teuer*	I'd like to buy...	*Ich möchte...kaufen*
hotel	*das Hotel*	for one night	*für eine Nacht*
room	*das Zimmer*	how much?...	*wieviel kostet es?*
I would like a	*Ich hätte gern*	breakfast	*das Frühstuck*
single	*ein Einzelzimmer*	toilet	*die Toilette*
double room	*ein Doppelzimmer*	key	*der Schlüssel*
with bath/shower	*mit Bad/Dusche*	lift/elevator	*der Aufzug*
restaurant	*das Restaurant*	white/red	*weiss/rot*
coffee house	*das Kaffeehaus*	water	*das Wasser*
pub	*die Gaststätte*	lunch	*Mittagessen*
menu	*die Speisekarte*	dinner	*Abendessen*
table	*der Tisch*	menu of the day	*Tagesmenü*
wine/beer	*der Wein/das Bier*	waiter	*Herr Ober*
airport	*der Flughafen*	bus	*der Bus*
railway station	*der Bahnhof*	tram	*die Strassenbahn*
subway station	*die U-bahn-station*	right/left	*rechts/links*
bus stop	*die Bushaltestelle*	straight on	*geradeaus*

Best places to see

1 Dürnstein

With its romantic castle ruins and breathtaking Danube views, the walled town of Dürnstein is one of the most photogenic spots in the Wachau region.

The village itself is tiny but picturesque. The 16th-century houses on Hauptstrasse with Renaissance balconies and projecting windows are especially appealing. Don't miss the Stiftskirche, the former

Augustinian monastery, with its exquisite blue-and-white baroque tower, erected in 1725.

It's a 15- to 30-minute climb from the Steiner Tor to the ruined fortress where King Richard the Lionheart of England was held captive by Leopold, Duke of Austria in 1193 – the two had fallen out during the Third Crusade. According to legend, Richard's minstrel, Blondel, set out to find his master and, on reaching the castle at Dürnstein, began to sing one of the king's favourite melodies. Richard recognized the tune and took up the refrain but, despite Blondel's efforts, continued to languish in jail for more than a year. He was finally released after the payment of a huge ransom. The castle was dismantled by the Swedes during the Thirty Years' War but there are outstanding views of the river valley from the ruins.

After sampling the famous local wine, *Grüner Veltliner*, you could explore other beauty spots in the region: Weissenkirchen (another wine-producing village), the Kuernringer castle ruins at Aggstein, the pilgrimage churches of Maria Langegg and Maria Taferl, and of course Melk Abbey (➤ 50–51).

✚ 9C ✉ 70km (43 miles) northwest of Vienna
🕐 Stiftskirche: Apr–Oct Mon–Sat 9–6, Sun 10–6 🚍 Dürnstein
ℹ Hauptstrasse 132 ☎ 0271 1200
🕐 Apr–Oct

2 Eisriesenwelt

www.eisriesenwelt.at

The 'World of the Ice Giants' is how the Austrians describe this extraordinary natural phenomenon – one of the largest ice cave networks on earth.

Allow at least half a day to visit to these shining ice caves. Before starting out you'll need a stout pair of shoes, a sweater and a pair of gloves – forget how warm it is on the outside, the temperature inside the caves hovers at around 0°C (32°F).

The route from Werfen allows for spectacular views of the surrounding countryside. The 5km-long (3-mile) mountain road climbs to the parking areas, from where it's a 15-minute walk to the cable-car. The footpath overlooks the Salzach Valley and the majestic Hohenwerfen Fortress. From the cable-car it's another 15- to 20-minute walk to the main entrance of the caves themselves, 1,640m (5,380ft) above the valley floor.

The guided tour lasts about 75 minutes. Visitors climb the steps to the gallery where the real show begins. The frozen waterfalls, glaciers, stalactites and ice curtains are lit to brilliant effect, giving the walls a bluish-white sheen. The caves extend for more than 42km (26 miles) from the western cliff of the Hochkogel and the walls are more than 20m (65ft) thick in places. Some of the more spectacular formations have fanciful names like 'Palace of the Ice Giants', 'Ice Queen's Veil' and 'The Cathedral'.

Werfen itself has a wonderful mountain setting and you may be tempted to stay the night. If so,

don't fail to sign up for the guided tour of the Hohenwerfen Fortress to see the Knights Hall, the torture chamber, the chapel with its fresco of the apocalypse, and the birds of prey that circle dramatically overhead.

✚ 4E ✉ A-5450 Werfen, 30km (18 miles) south of Salzburg ☎ 06468 5248 🕓 Tours May, Jun, Sep daily 9:30–3:30 hourly; Jul–Aug daily 9:30–4:30 hourly ✋ Expensive (all inclusive ticket available) 🍴 Restaurant (€€) 🚌 Eisriesenwelt-Linie, May–Oct approx 2-hourly (more frequently if demand); cable-car May, Jun, Sep–early Oct daily 9–5; Jul–Aug daily 9–6 ❓ Photography and filming are forbidden inside the caves

3 Hallstatt

www.hallstatt.net

Described in the 19th century as 'the loveliest lakeside village in the world', Hallstatt lies at the heart of the scenic Salzkammergut 'lake district'.

The word *Salz* means 'salt' and it was this commodity that made Hallstatt a thriving commercial centre before Rome was even thought of. The prehistoric finds, including bronze dishes from the Danube, amber from northern Germany, glass from Italy and ivory from Africa, were considered so important that the era from 800 to 400BC is now universally known as the 'Hallstatt Period'.

The village is wedged between the Hallstätter See and the Dachstein Mountains – there's no room for a railway line, so you have to travel across the lake by boat. Hallstatt's 16th-century parish church (Pfarrkirche) is the focal point of an annual Corpus Christi procession at the end of May. Note the colourful frescoes over the porch and don't miss the gorgeous winged altarpiece on the Gothic high altar. The charnel house next door is a no-holds-barred *memento mori*, with row upon row of neatly arranged skulls and bones,

many of them painted and inscribed with names and dates.

A funicular will take you 350m (1,148ft) above the village to the oldest working **salt mines** in the world, first exploited in the neolithic era. The guided tour is an absolute must. Visitors get protective clothing, then board the mine train which trundles 2km (1.2 miles) into the Christina tunnel. You see a film on the history of the mine, slide down a wooden chute to an underground lake, look down on an illuminated crater and walk the final 185m (600ft) to the train and daylight. You can then finish off with a meal in the Rudolfsturm, a medieval tower built in 1284 to protect the mine.

✚ 5E 🖂 50km (31 miles) southeast of Salzburg 🚉 Hallstatt, then ferry
🚢 Schiffahrt Hemetsberger ☎ 06134 8228 (ferry from train and lake trips)
❷ Corpus Christi lake festival (➤ 24)
ℹ Seestrasse 169 ☎ 06134 8208

Salzbergwerk (salt mines)
☎ 06132 2002400 🕐 Apr–Sep daily 9:30–4:30; Oct daily 9:30–3 ✋ Expensive
🍴 Berggasthof Rudolfsturm (€€€; ➤ 159) ❷ Guided tours Apr–Oct daily 9–4:30 (allow 2 hours)

4 Hohe Tauern

The largest national park in central Europe, with an area of nearly 1,800sq km (695sq miles), Hohe Tauern is a beautiful and unspoiled natural landscape.

If you're intending to explore the park for any length of time, Zell am See (➤ 179), Lienz, Bad Gastein and Matrei make attractive and convenient bases. The tourist offices can provide you with information about free parking, taxi shuttles, visitors centres, overnight refuges and the all-important route maps. The park authorities have come up with more than 80 tour suggestions – each includes a summary of what you're likely to see, as well as information

about parking, access and walking times. Besides walking and hiking, activities offered include rock climbing, kayaking, alpine rafting and fishing.

The hiking trails (all clearly marked and signposted) include a number of specially designated 'family routes' which explain the particular natural environment and the underlying ecosystem. One of the more unusual is the Römerstrasse, a pack trail forged by Roman soldiers 2,000 years ago to secure the trade in wine and salt.

Wherever you go the scenery ranges from the stunning to the spectacular: gorges and ravines, waterfalls and mountain lakes, alpine meadows ablaze with wild flowers, virgin forests of larch and stone pine. On your travels you may encounter alpine salamanders, vultures, golden and sea eagles, marmots, red deer, ibex and chamois.

Private cars are prohibited from Hohe Tauern, with the exception of major through roads. The other star attraction is the Krimml Waterfall, easily accessed from Zell am See.

🚩 16J ✉ 60km (37 miles) south of Salzburg ☎ 04875 5112 🕐 All year 🖐 Free entry to park 🍴 Restaurants (€€–€€€) 🚊 Zell am See, Lienz, Mallnitz

ℹ Zell am See (➤ 179); Badgastein ✉ Kaiser-Franz-Josef-Strasse ☎ 06434 2531; Lienz ✉ Europlatz 1 ☎ 04852 6526-5; Matrei ✉ Rauterplatz 1 ☎ 04875 6527-0

5 Kitzbühel

www.tirol.at/kitzbuehel

One of Austria's oldest and most glamorous ski resorts, Kitzbühel also offers wonderful opportunities for walking and cycling in summer.

Kitzbühel's prosperity initially derived from silver and copper mining. It was only at the end of the 19th century with the arrival of the first party of Norwegian skiers that the town discovered an even more lucrative source of income. The wooded valley provides an attractive backdrop to the local sights – a couple of historic churches, as well as several rows of handsome 16th- and 17th-century burghers' houses, all brightly painted. Prices are steep during the skiing season, especially in the glitziest bars and discos, but the increasing number of package tourists has introduced a welcome note of realism.

Most skiers head for the Kitzbüheler Horn (1,996m/6,549ft) and the Hahnenkamm (1,600m/5,250ft). There are more than 60 runs, mainly suited to beginners and intermediates, although there are some difficult runs on the Hahnenkamm. Other winter sports available include cross-country skiing, snowboarding and tobogganing.

A major attraction in the summer is the Alpine Flower Garden on the Kitzbüheler Horn, a riot of colour with 120 different species. The tourist office provides maps and leaflets detailing cycle routes and more than 40 walks through the lush Alpine meadows. You can also take a ride up the Hahnenkamm to visit the **Cable-Car Museum.**

🚋 2E ⊠ 80km (50 miles) east of Innsbruck 🚆 Kitzbühel
🚌 Bus to ski fields; cable-car services to the peaks via the Bergbahn ❓ World Cup skiing Jan; open-air concerts (Jul, Aug)
ℹ Hinterstadt 18 ☎ 05356 7770

Cable-Car Museum
⊠ Hahnenkamm Mountain Station 🕐 Daily 10–5

6 Kunsthistorisches Museum, Vienna

www.khm.at

This fabulous art collection, one of the most important in the world, was moved from the Belvedere to its present premises in 1891.

Designed by Gottfried Semper and Karl Hasenauer, the Kunsthistorisches Museum is an imposing work of architecture. On the ground floor you'll find the Oriental and Egyptian collections, Greek and Roman antiquities, sculpture and decorative arts. As there are more than 4km (2.5 miles) of galleries, you'll need to be selective – pick up a copy of the museum layout before you set off.

The picture gallery is on the first floor and the collection shows Habsburg treasures and the territories over which they ruled. The Netherlands are especially well represented – there are more paintings by Pieter

Brueghel the Elder here than anywhere else in the world. They include the masterpieces *Hunters in the Snow, Peasant Wedding, Children's Games* and the satirical *Battle between Carnival and Lent.* Other highlights among the Dutch and Flemish Old Masters are a *Crucifixion* triptych by Rogier van der Weyden, several portraits by Rembrandt (including one of his mother) and an entire room of Van Dycks.

The scale and ambition of Rubens' altarpieces will take your breath away. Many of the Italian paintings were acquired in the 17th century by Archduke Leopold Wilhelm. Rome is represented by Raphael, Venice by Bellini, Tintoretto and Titian – only the Prado in Madrid has more paintings by this artist.

✚ *Wien 4d* ✉ Maria-Theresien-Platz/Burgring 5
☎ 01 52524-0 🕐 Tue–Wed, Fri–Sun 10–6, Thu 10–9
✋ Moderate 🍴 Café on first floor (€€) 🚇 Volkstheater, MuseumsQuartier 🚌 1, 2, 2A, D, J, 57A

7 Maria Wörth and Wörther See

Gustav Mahler was inspired to write some of his greatest music while vacationing on the shores of this beautiful inland lake.

Mahler was especially taken with Maria Wörth and its idyllic setting on a peninsula reaching out into the lake. His villa lies hidden among the woods at Maiernigg, near Klagenfurt (► 150–151) – the cabin where he worked each summer is open to visitors. The Karawanken Alps stretch into the distance, while the two pilgrimage churches here are 'must sees' for their medieval frescoes and statuary. Boat excursions leave from Klagenfurt for Maria Wörth and several other destinations along the lake. For romantics there are moonlight cruises on board the *Thalia*, a restored 1908 passenger steamer.

The promenade at Pörtschach is perfect for an evening stroll after a day spent on the beach (you can swim as early as May here) while the nightlife rivals that of Velden, the busiest of the resorts. Windsurfing, sailing and water skiing are all possible in Velden but if the crowds begin to pall, leave the boutiques and café terraces behind for **Wildpark Rosegg**, a wildlife park with white wolves, lynx, bison and birds of prey.

Finding somewhere to stay isn't a problem. If money is no object, consider one of the converted lakeside villas built around the turn of the 20th century for the Viennese business élite. More economical alternatives include Krumpendorf, a spa near Velden, or Reifnitz, a quiet little town only a few kilometres' drive from the 850m-high (2,789ft)

Pyramidenkogel (observation tower) with unbeatable views of the Carinthian countryside, weather permitting.

✚ 19K ✉ 100km (62 miles) west of Graz 🚆 Klagenfurt, Pörtschach, Velden 🚢 Wörther See Schiffahrt, Klagenfurt ☎ 0463 21155, round trip to Velden 3 hours 45 minutes 🛈 Klagenfurt (➤ 151); Pörtschach ✉ Hauptstrasse 153 ☎ 04272 2354

Wildpark Rosegg
✉ 5km (3 miles) south of Velden ☎ 04274 52357
🕓 Apr–Oct daily 9–5; Jul–Aug daily 9–6 ✋ Moderate
Pyramidenkogel
🕓 Apr, Oct daily 10–6; May, Sep 9–7; Jun 9–8; Jul, Aug 9–9

8 Melk

Melk has been an important spiritual and cultural centre for more than 1,000 years. The town is famous for its Benedictine abbey, founded in 1089.

Melk Abbey, a spectacular masterpiece of baroque architecture, is perched on a rocky promontory high above the Danube. It was renowned as a medieval seat of learning and inspired Umberto Eco's

detective novel *The Name of the Rose* (Melk too was destroyed by fire, on more than one occasion).

Highlights of the guided tour include the abbey church, the library, the Marmorsaal (Marble Hall) and the superb Kaiserstiege (Imperial Staircase) which paves the way for the 190m-long (620ft) gallery known as the Kaisergang. The church's sumptuous interior, with its gilded stucco embelishments, Italianate paintings, carved pulpit and magnificent dome, takes the breath away. The monastic library contains more than 80,000 books, as well as illuminated manuscripts dating back to the 12th century. The ceiling fresco by Paul Troger is a masterpiece. The Marble Hall is also impressive, especially when you realize that the columns are *faux-marbre* and not the genuine article. Among the guests entertained here are Pope Pius VI, Empress Maria Theresa and Napoleon.

The town, some 50m (165ft) below the monastery, has some quaint houses including the former monastery tavern, a beautifully preserved Renaissance post office, fortified towers and a 15th-century parish church with an unusual calvary (open-air representation of the crucifixion).

✚ 8C ✉ 85km (53 miles) west of Vienna 🚊 Emmersdorf an der Donau (3km/2 miles) ❓ Melk Summer Festival (theatre); baroque music at Whitsun
ℹ️ Babenbergerstrasse 1 ☎ 02752 5230732

Melk Abbey
✉ Abt Berthold Dietmayr-Strasse 1 ☎ 02752 555225/ 555232 (guided tours) 🕐 Apr–Oct daily 9–4:30; May–Sep until 5:30 💰 Moderate 🍴 Restaurant (€€)

9 Schloss Schönbrunn, Vienna

www.schoenbrunn.at

This palatial summer residence, built by Maria Theresa between 1743 and 1749, is actually a scaled-down version of an earlier, more ambitious design.

Schönbrunn takes its name from the 'beautiful spring' discovered here by Emperor Matthias in the 17th century. Fischer von Erlach's extravagant plans for the palace, intended to rival Versailles, were abandoned when Maria Theresa called for a summer residence that would serve as a home for her consort and their 16 children. Even so, there are 1,441 rooms!

The 'Grand Tour' takes in the apartments of Emperor Franz-Josef and Empress Elizabeth, the ceremonial and state halls and audience chambers of Maria Theresa. The interiors are an artistic treasure house – frescoes, *trompe l'oeil* paintings, marquetry, lacquer work, gilded mirrors, Gobelin tapestries, marble and crystal. The most impressive of Schönbrunn's reception rooms is the Large Gallery – 43m (140ft) long and 10m (33ft) high.

Yet for all the pomp and circumstance of court ceremony many of the rooms were actually lived in, and herein lies the real interest. The round Chinese Room, for example, has a dumb waiter for intimate private dinners and a secret staircase used by Maria Theresa for assignations with her lover, the Austrian chancellor. You can also see the Hall of Mirrors where the Empress took the six-year-old

Mozart on to her lap, and the room belonging to the most famous of her daughters, Marie Antoinette.

After the tour, spend some time in the immaculate formal gardens and landscaped park. There are magnificent views of Vienna from the triumphal gate known as the Gloriette. There's also the world's oldest surviving zoo and a Coach Museum with more than 100 ceremonial coaches, sedan chairs and prams, dating back to 1690. If you leave via the Hietzing exit you'll see the emperor's private railway station.

✚ *Wien 1f* ✉ Schönbrunner Schlossstrasse 47 ☎ 01 81113 239 🕐 Palace: Apr–Jun, Sep, Oct daily 8:30–5; Jul–Aug daily 8:30–6; Nov–Mar daily 8:30–4.30. Coach Museum: Apr–Oct daily 9–6; Nov–Mar Tue–Sun 10–4. Zoo: summer daily 9–6:30, winter daily 9–sunset. Park: daily 6–sunset 🎫 Expensive 🍴 Café and Tirolean restaurant (€€) 🚇 Schönbrunn, Hietzing 🚌 10, 10A, 58 ❓ Imperial Tour 22 rooms (35 mins); Grand Tour 40 rooms (50 mins). Audioguide available

10 Vienna's MuseumsQuartier

www.mqw.at

The most exciting addition to Vienna's rich cultural heritage is the creation of one of the world's largest museum districts, with a dozen or more galleries and halls.

On the edge of the old city, the MuseumsQuartier Wien opened in June 2001. The architecture ranges from the recycled Court Stables to the latest contemporary design. There is something for everyone; the **Zoom Kindermuseum** (where kids can play at being a movie director), Hall E and G (two performance spaces), **Tanzquartier Wien** (a centre for contemporary dance) and the Art Cult Centre, devoted to the history of tobacco.

The heart of the area is provided by three major museums: the Leopold, MUMOK and the Kunsthalle. The **Leopold Museum** is named for the connoisseur who donated his collection of 5,000 Austrian art works to the nation. As well as paintings by Oskar Kokoschka and Gustav Klimt, there is the world's largest collection of Egon Schiele. Alongside treasures from Japan, China, India and Africa is early 20th-century Viennese furniture, with designs by Adolf Loos, Otto Wagner and Josef Hoffmann.

The **Kunsthalle** is a space dedicated to rotating exhibitions. Then there is **MUMOK** (MUseum MOderner Kunst), the five-floor Museum of Modern Art, with excellent examples of Picasso,

Warhol and Klee. But the MuseumsQuartier, or MuQua (Moo-Kvah) as the locals have nicknamed it, is much more than an intellectual gathering place. Most of the buildings house a museum shop or art bookshop, as well as a trendy café, bar or restaurant. The Viennese are using them as a novel place to feed the body as well as the mind.

✚ *Wien 4d* ✉ Museumsplatz 1 ☎ 01 523 5881 ext 1730 ⊕ Visitor Centre: daily 10–7 🍽 Cafés/restaurants (€) Ⓜ MuseumsQuartier, Volkstheater 🚌 2A, 48A; tram 49

Zoom Kindermuseum
☎ 01 524 7908; www.kindermuseum.at
⊕ Mon–Fri 8:30–5, Sat–Sun 10–5:30

Tanzquartier Wien
☎ 01 581 3591

Leopold Museum
☎ 01 525 700; www.leopoldmuseum.at
⊕ Daily 10–6 (Thu until 9pm)

Kunsthalle
☎ 01 521 890; www.kunsthallewien.at
⊕ Daily 10–7 (Thu 10–10)

MUMOK
☎ 01525 00; www.mumok.at ⊕ Tue–Sun 10–6, Thu 10–9

Best things to do

Good places to have lunch

Berggasthof Rudolfsturm (€€€)
Enjoy the regional specialities
and the fine views over the
Hallstätter See.
✉ Salzberg 1, Hallstatt (cable-car
terminus) ☎ 06134 20677

Gasthof zur Linde (€€)
Specializes in game and locally
caught trout.
✉ Hauptplatz, Laaben bei
Neulengbach, Vienna Woods
☎ 02774 8378

Jell (€€)
A quaint traditional place with
lots of rustic charm which has
been serving tasty local dishes
since 1897.
✉ Hoher Markt 8–9, Krems an der
Donau ☎ 02732 82345

Landhauskeller (€€€)
Enjoy a traditional Styrian lunch
in the historic centre.
✉ Schmiedgasse 9, Graz
☎ 0316 830276

Museum der Moderne (€€)
Outstanding views of Salzburg
from the café terrace.
✉ Am Mönchsberg 32, Salzburg
☎ 0662 8422 20403

Palmenhaus (€€)

Centrally located in the Burggarten, near the Albertina art museum.

✉ Burggarten 1, Vienna
☎ 01 533 1033

Schweizerhaus (€€)

Delicious haunches of meat in this garden-restaurant.

✉ Prater 116, Vienna
☎ 01 728 015213

See Restaurant (€€)

Watch the boats set out onto the Neusiedler See while you enjoy *Steckerl* (a local fish, usually barbecued).

✉ Am Seekanal 2, Rust
☎ 02685 3810

Stiftskeller (€€)

Authentic Tirolean inn, with an outdoor beer garden in summer.

✉ Stiftgasse 1, Innsbruck
☎ 0512 570706

Take a picnic with you to the beach at Klagenfurt and enjoy wonderful views of the Wörther See.

Places to take the children

Alpen Wildpark
A deer park with areas for petting animals, and wildlife exhibition.
✉ Feld am See, Carinthia ☎ 04246 2776 🕐 May–Sep daily 9–6; Oct 9–5
✋ Inexpensive

Haus der Natur
Huge museum complex, with a large aquarium, reptile house,
space hall and special exhibitions on mineralogy, geology etc.
✉ Museumsplatz 5, Salzburg ☎ 0662 842653 🕐 Daily 9–5 ✋ Moderate

Märchenpark
Leisure park with ghost castle, monorail, baby animals, life-size
fairy-tale characters and fairground rides.
✉ Am Rusterberg, St Margarethen, Neusiedler See ☎ 02685 60707
🕐 Apr–Sep daily 9–6 (attractions 10–6); Oct daily 9–5 ✋ Moderate

Marionettentheater
Puppet performances of famous operas (also well-known pieces
like *The Nutcracker* and *Peter and the Wolf*) for children over seven.
✉ Schwarzstrasse 24, Salzburg ☎ 0662 872406 🕐 Box office Mon–Sat 9–1
and 2 hours before each performance. Tickets also on sale at hotels

Minimundus
A park with scale models of some of the world's most famous
monuments. Play areas and swimming etc.
✉ Villacher Strasse 241, Klagenfurt ☎ 0463 21194 🕐 Apr, Oct daily 9–6;
May, Jun, Sep daily 9–7; Jul–Aug daily 9–8

Safari-und-Abenteuer Park Gänserndorf
A mixture of safari park and adventure park with acrobats,
daredevil acts, trampolines and kiddy rides.
✉ Siebenbrunnerstrasse, Gänserndorf, east of Vienna ☎ 02282 702610
🕐 Apr–Oct daily 9:30–5:30, until 7:30 summer ✋ Moderate (all-inclusive)

Seegrotte

Europe's largest underground lake grotto with boat trips.

 Grutschgasse 2A, Hinterbrühl bei Wien 02236 26364 Apr–Oct daily 9–5; Nov–Mar Mon–Fri 9–12, 1–3, Sat, Sun 9–3:30 Expensive

Styrassic Park

Life-sized dinosaur models, eggs and so on in wooded parkland. Children's play area and restaurant.

Dinoplatz 1, Bad Gleichenberg, near Graz 03159 28750 Apr–Sep daily 9–5; Mar, Oct daily 9–4 Moderate

Wildpark Hochkreut

A fine collection of mountain wildlife – sheep and deer, goats and ponies, yaks and mouflon (wild sheep). Rides for children and birdsong trail.

Aurachberg 60, Neukirchen bei Altmünster 07618 8205 Easter–Oct daily 9–6 Inexpensive

Zwergenpark

Gnome garden complete with miniature railway.

Gurk, Carinthia 04266 8077 May–Jun daily 11–4; Jul–late Aug daily 10–6; late Aug to mid-Sep daily 11–4 Inexpensive

Best souvenir shops

GRAZ
Steirisches Heimatwerk
Handicraft shop with everything from dolls with embroidered costumes to folk outfits, inscribed glassware and tankards, porcelain and ornaments.
✉ Sporgasse 23 ☎ 0316 827106

GMUNDEN
Gmundner Keramik
First produced in the 16th century, Gmunden pottery is famous for its distinctive green swirls and curlicues on a white base.
✉ Keramikstrasse 24 ☎ 07612 7860

HALLSTATT
Keramik Hallstatt
Waterfront shop selling an excellent range of handmade, painted and decorated ceramics.
✉ Wolfengasse 107 ☎ 06134 8460

INNSBRUCK
Swarovski
You can buy glassware, jewellery and objects made of crystal such as candle-holders, swans, clocks, ships, keyrings etc. There are also regular glass-blowing displays.
✉ Kristallweltenstrasse 1, Wattens ☎ 05224 51080
✉ Crystal Gallery, Herzog-Friedrich-Strasse 39, Innsbruck ☎ 051 573100

SALZBURG
Salzburger Heimatwerk
Locally produced ceramics, glassware, candles, CDs and many other gifts for sale at this newly opened outlet.
✉ Residenzplatz 9 ☎ 0662 844110

VIENNA
Augarten
Manufacturers of Viennese porcelain since 1718; there are occasional thematic exhibitions in the store.

✉ Graben/Stock-Im-Eisen-Platz 3 ☎ 01 512 1494

Lobmeyr
This is one of Austria's most famous purveyors of glassware, specializing in crystal chandeliers. Also sells porcelain and silverware.

✉ Kärntnerstrasse 26 ☎ 01 512 0508 🕐 Closed Sat pm, Sun

Schloss Schönbrunn Museum Shop
Novelty watches, books, cards, CDs, videos and other themed merchandise.

✉ Schönbrunner Schlossstrasse 47 ☎ 01 811130

Trachten Tostmann
Specializes in Austrian handicrafts and costumes; just up from the Burgtheater.

✉ Schottengasse 3a ☎ 01 533 5331

ZELL AM SEE
Anna Frank
Swarovski silver crystal and other glassware and ceramic items are on sale in this local shop. There's also a branch in the Vogtturm.

✉ Seegasse 9 ☎ 06542 72574

Top activities

Cycling: Away from the mountains, this is one of the best ways of getting around and of enjoying the countryside on the thousands of kilometres of marked tracks.

Rafting: The fast-flowing rivers of the Tirol, Salzburg and Styria are increasingly popular with rafting enthusiasts; take a local guide.

Skiing, or snowboarding, tobogganing, ice skating and curling, at a top winter sports resort.

Swimming: Austria has more than 2,000 lakes, many of which are well suited to swimming. The water in the Wörther See is enticingly warm, even in May.

Walking: Many of the hills and mountain areas have well-marked paths and signposts giving you the distance and time to reach the next destination.

Best views

Melk Abbey from the Danube, perched on a bluff 50m (165ft) above the river.

The Loisach Valley and the Lechtal Alps from Zugspitzkamm (2,805m/9,203ft), reached by cable-car from Obermoos.

Salzburg from the terrace of the Hohensalzburg castle.

Vienna from the giant Ferris wheel in the Prater (➤ 92–93).

Wachau Valley from Burg Aggstein, 300m (985ft) above the river.

Top scenic routes

● The train from Attnang-Puchheim to Hallstatt follows the banks of the Traunsee to Bad Ischl and on to the Hallstätter See.

● The spectacular Semmering Pass between Mürzzuschlag and Gloggnitz was one of the first rail routes over the Alps, completed in 1854.

● The 30km (18-mile) run between Krems and Melk in the Wachau is one of the most scenic train journeys in Austria.

● En route to Innsbruck, the train from Zell am See climbs through the majestic Kitzbüheler Alpen before making the descent to the Inn valley.

● The boat cruise from Klagenfurt to Velden is a leisurely way of exploring the lakeside resorts of the Wörther See.

● The combination of funicular and two-stage cable-car ride from Innsbruck to the Hafelekar peak (2,334m/7,658ft) is the ideal way to view the Inn valley and surrounding countryside.

● The Murtalbahn narrow-gauge railway in the Mur valley runs a steam service between Unzmarkt and Tamsweg in summer (➤ 123).

● Motorists in the Paznauntal will enjoy the wonderful mountain drive on the Partenen to Galtür Road (also known as the Silvrettastrasse) – open May to November.

● There are breathtaking views of Bodensee from the cable-car to the summit of the Pfänder mountain (1,063m/3,488ft).

● The scenic steam railway from Mariazell goes to Erlaufsee, a pretty lake 3km (2 miles) to the northwest.

Best museums

Heeresgeschichtliches Museum: The main draw at Vienna's Military History Museum is the room dedicated to the 1914 assassination of Archduke Ferdinand d'Este in Sarajevo, an event which lit the blue touch paper of World War I. His bullet-riddled car and coat are gruesome reminders of those monumentous days.
✉ Arsenal ☎ 79561-0 🕐 9–5

Kunsthistorisches Museum, Vienna: A magnificent building housing what amounts to one of the world's top art collections (➤ 46–47).

Landesmuseum Joanneum, Graz: This is Austria's oldest museum occupying 19 sites around the city.
✉ Raubergasse 10 ☎ 80179740 🕐 Limited hours due to renovation

Lentos Kunstmuseum, Linz: One of Austria's most cutting-edge exhibition spaces houses a top-notch show of contemporary artworks, including pieces by Warhol, Klimt, Schiele and Kokoschka.
✉ Ernst-Koref-Promenade 1 ☎ 7327070 🕐 10–6

Leopold Museum, Vienna: The now state-owned collection of Rudolf Leopold is housed in a purpose-built museum and contains 5,266 paintings valued at over £300 million. Viennese favourites Klimt, Schiele and Kokoschka are well represented.
✉ Museumsplatz 1 ☎ 52570 🕐 10–6

Mozart Wohnhaus, Salzburg: This exhibition occupying the apartment which the Mozarts rented between 1783 and 1780 is one of Salzburg's top attractions (➤ 140–141).

Museum Moderner Kunst (MUMOK), Vienna: Austria's premier exhibition of modern art with over 9,000 works on rotating display. Anyone with even a passing interest in pop art, cubism or

nouveau realism should
not let this one pass by.
✉ Museumsplatz 1 ☎ 52500
🕐 10–6

**MuseumsQuartier,
Vienna:** The unrivalled star
of Austria's museum world
and an unmissable stop on
every Vienna itinerary
(➤ 54–55).

**Österreichisches
Museum fur Angewandte
Kunst (MAK), Vienna:** The
Museum of Applied Art
exhibits glass, textiles,
porcelain, jewellery and
many other decorative
items in a 19th-century
neo-Renaissance edifice.
It has one of the best
museum shops around and
a superb cafe (➤ 90).

Salzburg Museum:
Opened in 2007, Salzburg's
city museum housed in the
Neue Residenz palace
traces the city's history
from medieval times.
✉ Mozartplatz 1 ☎ 620808
🕐 Tue–Sun 9–5

Best nightlife

GRAZ
Casino Graz
French and American roulette, blackjack, baccarat and punto banco. Passport required.

✉ Landhausgasse 10 ☎ 0316 832578 🕐 Daily from 3pm

Miles Jazz Bar
The most popular jazz club in jazz-crazed Graz. Features acts from around the world.

✉ Mariahilferstrasse 24 ☎ 0699 105 100 47 🕐 Wed–Sat 7pm–2am

INNSBRUCK
Couch Club
DJs play house and hip hop in the old town.

✉ Anichstrasse 7 ☎ 0699 1188 9039

Filou
Haunt of the 'beautiful people', this disco-bar has a pleasant garden which closes at 10pm.

✉ Stiftgasse 12 ☎ 0512 580256 🕐 Daily 10pm–5am

SALZBURG
Casino Salzburg
Try your luck at French and American roulette, blackjack, poker, red dog, seven eleven; also slot machines. Be sure not to forget your passport.

✉ Schloss Klessheim ☎ 0662 854455 🕐 Daily from 3pm 🚌 Shuttle service from town centre

Chez Roland
A fun cellar bar with many local wines.

✉ Giselkai 15 ☎ 0662 874335 🕐 Daily 7:30pm–4am

VIENNA

Casino Wien

Gamble the night away in suitably palatial surroundings.

✉ Kärntnerstrasse 41 ☎ 01 512 4836 🕓 Daily from 3pm

Flex

One of the grooviest clubs in the city, featuring top DJs, live gigs and all the latest sounds.

✉ Donaukanal Augartenbrücke ☎ 01 533 7525 🕓 Daily 8pm–4am
🚇 Schottenring

Jazzland

Popular trad-jazz scene in a Bermuda Triangle cellar.

✉ Franz-Josefs-Kai 29 ☎ 01 533 2575 🕓 Mon–Sat 7:30pm–2am
🚇 Schwedenplatz

Planter's Club

Colonial-style bar popular with celebrities. More than 1,500 spirits to chose from, including 450 single malts.

✉ Zelinkagasse 4 ☎ 01 533 339315 🕓 Daily 5pm–4am 🚇 Schottenring

Opera and classical music

GRAZ
Opera Haus (Opera House)
A varied schedule of opera and ballet is staged in this grandiose 19th-century building. Some of the productions are quite progressive, and tickets are fairly easy to come by throughout the season.

✉ Kaiser-Josef-Platz 10 ☎ 0316 8000

INNSBRUCK
Tiroler Landestheater
The provincial theatre stages classical operas (Mozart, Verdi etc) as well as operettas and musicals.

✉ Rennweg 2 ☎ 0512 520744

SALZBURG
Hohensalzburg
Concerts are held in the fortress throughout the year – come for chamber music, or Advent and Christmas concerts, in the state apartments.

✉ Salzburg ☎ 0662 842430-20 (information and tickets)

Schloss Mirabell
The emphasis here is on chamber music, especially, though not exclusively, works by Mozart.

✉ Theatergasse 2 ☎ 0662 848586

VIENNA

Bösendorfer Saal
Named after Vienna's most celebrated dynasty of piano makers, a popular venue for chamber music concerts.

✉ Graf-Starhemberg-Gasse 14 ☎ 01 504 665144 Ⓤ Taubstummengasse

Kursalon
This is the main venue for Strauss programmes and other popular concerts.

✉ Johannesgasse 33 ☎ 01 513 2477 Ⓤ Stadtpark

Musikverein
Very much a Viennese institution, the Musikverein has two concert halls: the Grosser Saal, home of the Vienna Philharmonic Orchestra, and the Brahmssaal (used mainly for chamber music).

✉ Bösendorferstrasse 12 ☎ 01 505 8190 Ⓤ Karlsplatz

Staatsoper (State Opera)
One of the world's leading opera stages with a mainly conservative repertoire (Mozart, Verdi etc). Difficult to get tickets.

✉ Opernring 2 ☎ 51444 7880 Ⓤ Oper

Volksoper
More light-hearted opera and operettas, performed to the same high standard as the State Opera.

✉ Währingerstrasse 78 ☎ 01 51444 3670 Ⓤ Volksoper

Wiener Kammeroper
The Viennese Chamber Opera is where many of the shining lights of the Volksoper and Staatsoper start out. The schedule includes many lesser-known operas, sometimes abridged.

✉ Fleischmarkt 24 ☎ 01 512 0100-77 Ⓤ Schwedenplatz

around Vienna

From Stephansplatz cross Stock-im-Eisen-Platz.

On arriving in Vienna (Wien) apprentice metalsmiths would hammer a nail into a tree trunk for luck, hence Stock-im-Eisen (nail-studded stump).

Stroll up the Graben, with its splendid 19th-century buildings, passing the exuberant Pest Saüle (Plague Column), erected in 1693, and the Peterskirche (► 90–91). Turn left into Kohlmarkt, with Demel's pâtisserie (► 103) on your right.

At the end of Kohlmarkt, the classical facade of the Michaelerkirche contrasts with its simple Gothic interior.

The grisly remains of wealthy parishioners can be seen in open coffins in the crypt.

From Michaelerplatz take Schauflergasse, turning right into Minoritenplatz. Beyond the 14th-century Minoritenkirche turn left at Bankgasse to the Burgtheater.

Part of the Ringstrasse project, initiated in 1857, the Burgtheater and the neo-Gothic Rathaus opposite are typical of the over-blown architecture of the late imperial period. On the corner of Dr-Karl-Lueger-Ring is Café Landtmann, where you can ponder the wonders of 19th-century town planning over a leisurely lunch.

Walk past the theatre, then through the rose gardens of the Volksgarten. At the end is the Hofburg (➤ 86–87). Continue to Burg Tor. On your right is the Kunsthistorisches Museum (➤ 46–47). Turn left and walk through to the Inner Courtyard, then turn right under the Schweizer Tor to Josefsplatz, the entrance to the Spanische Hofreitschule (Spanish Riding School; ➤ 98) and the Augustinerkirche. Walk down Augustinerstrasse, then turn left into Tegetthofstrasse and Neuer Markt.

On the corner of the square is the Kapuzinergruft (➤ 88), while in the centre stands a copy of Georg Raphael Donner's splendid Providence Fountain of 1739. The original is in Schloss Belvedere (➤ 94–95).

Distance 2.5km (1.5 miles)
Time 2–6 hours depending on which sights you visit
Start point Stephansplatz ✚ *Wien 5d* 🚇 Stephansdom
End point Neuer Markt ✚ *Wien 5d* 🚇 Oper
Lunch Café Landtmann (➤ 103)

Best food and drink shops

GRAZ
Hofbäckerei Edegger-Tax
Once the imperial bakery – hence the splendid carved crest above the doorway – this building dates from 1569. As well as the bakery, there's a small café where you can sample *Hofkaffée*, the speciality of the house – a coffee with egg liqueur, whipped cream and chocolate.

✉ Hofgasse 6 ☎ 0316 830230 🕐 Mon–Fri 6am–8pm, Sat 6–3

INNSBRUCK
Spezialitäten aus der Stiftgasse
Visit this vaulted cellar to shop for quality Austrian wines and brandies.

✉ Stiftgasse 2 ☎ 0512 576580 🕐 Mon–Fri 9:30–6:30

SALZBURG
Reber
The place to buy the original *Mozartkugeln* (Mozart balls) truffles, pralines and other sweet-toothed delights.

✉ Griessgasse 3 ☎ 0662 846851 🕐 Mon–Fri 10–6, Sat 9:30–6

R F Azwanger
Centrally located grocery store selling all kinds of goodies from the Alps, including pickles, chocolate bars, marmalades and alcohol distilled and fermented in the country.

✉ Getreidegasse 15 ☎ 0662 843394 🕐 Mon–Fri 10–6, Sat 9:30–4

VIENNA
Confiserie Walter Heindl
Sellers of the famous *Mozartkugeln* chocolates as well as other delights, including *Sissi Taler* (made from apricot marzipan and chocolate cream).

✉ Rotenturmstrasse 16 (corner of Fleischmarkt) ☎ 01 512 8522

Demmers Teehaus
Although Vienna is more famous for its coffee, there's no shortage of customers at this popular tea shop. There's a salon upstairs where you can imbibe.

✉ Mölker Bastei 5 ☎ 01 533 5995 🕐 Mon–Wed, Fri 9–6:30, Thu 9–8, Sat 9–12:30

Julius Meinl am Graben
Incorporates a restaurant, wine bar, coffee house and delicatessen in the heart of Vienna.

✉ Grabe 19 ☎ 01 532 3334 🕐 Closed Sun

Vinothek Bei Der Piaristenkirche
The place to buy Austrian wines including *Grüner Veltliner*, *Weissburgunder* and *Riesling*.

✉ Piaristengasse 54 ☎ 01 440 3094 🕐 Mon–Fri 3–6

Wienwein
An exquisite array of wines from the vineyards around Vienna by winegrowers Christ, Edlmoser, Wieninger and Zahel.

✉ Stammersdorfer Strasse 80 ☎ 01 290 1012

Best places to stay

DÜRNSTEIN
Hotel Schloss Dürnstein (€€€)
This luxury hotel, with indoor and outdoor swimming pools and sauna, occupies a 17th-century castle. Magnificent views of the Danube.

✉ Dürnstein 2 ☎ 02711 212; www.schloss.at

GRAZ
Hotel Schlossberg (€€€)
Elegantly furnished hotel with an ideal location between the Schlossberg and the main square. Sauna, solarium, fitness room and a rooftop swimming pool with garden. There's underground parking.

✉ Kaiser-Franz-Josef-Kai 30 ☎ 0316 8070; www.schlossberg-hotel.at

HALLSTATT
Bräugasthof Hallstatt (€)
Already on the map in 1472, this large hotel with comfortable rooms overlooks the lake. Terrace restaurant offering fish specialities.

✉ Seestrasse 120 ☎ 06134 8221; www.brauhaus-lobisser.com

INNSBRUCK
Goldener Adler (€€)
Innsbruck's most famous hotel, on a beautiful medieval street, has played host to royalty and celebrities, most notably Mozart and Goethe. Most of the rooms are spacious and you can choose to dine at one of two quality restaurants.

✉ Herzog-Friedrich-Strasse 6 ☎ 0512 571111; www.bestwestern.at

Hotel-Gasthof Bierwirt (€€€)
Hotel-pension in chalet-type building. Restaurant offering Tirolean specialities.

✉ Bichlweg 2 ☎ 0512 342143; www.bierwirt.com

NEUSIEDLER SEE
Romantik-Purbachhof (€€)
This beautifully restored wine-grower's house, dating from the 16th century, is a delight with simply furnished rooms and a sunny courtyard for lingering breakfasts.

✉ Schulgasse 14, Purbach ☎ 02683 5564; www.tiscover.at/purbachhof

SALZBURG
Goldener Hirsch (€€€)
Mozart himself may have been familiar with 'The Golden Stag', a venerable building dating from around 1400. There is an extra charge for breakfast.

✉ Getreidegasse 37 ☎ 0662 80840; www.goldenerhirsch.com

VIENNA
Hotel Sacher (€€€)
A Viennese institution featuring the luxury of former Imperial times.

✉ Philharmonikerstrasse 4 ☎ 01 514560; www.sacher.com Ⓟ Karlsplatz

Im Palais Schwarzenberg (€€€)
This luxury hotel, standing in its own park, occupies one of the best spots in the city.

✉ Schwarzenbergplatz 9 ☎ 01 798 4515; www.palais-schwarzenberg.com Ⓟ Karlsplatz

WÖRTHER SEE
Hubertushof (€€–€€€)
A pair of converted turn-of-the-20th-century villas overlooking the lake with indoor pool and sauna.

✉ Europaplatz 1, Velden ☎ 04274 26760; www.hubertus-hof.info

Exploring

From the Tirolean Alps to the rolling hills and vineyards of Burgenland, Austria is a land of contrasts with wonderful opportunities for rambling, hiking, bird-watching, picnicking and generally making the most of the peace and quiet.

And as a sports mecca, attracting enthusiasts from all over the world, Austria is second to none. Excellent facilities and warm hospitality make it a first choice for winter sports enthusiasts, while in the summer you can try everything from rock climbing to river rafting.

As you'll soon discover, each of Austria's nine provinces has a distinct identity, and the fact that its peoples are so diverse may come as a surprise. It's this variety that makes Austria so special: one country, many facets.

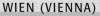

Wien (Vienna)

Music and dancing have always been an integral part of the Viennese way of life. It's no accident that the waltz, queen of ballroom dances, originated in this most elegant and stylish of cities and hardly surprising that the Strausses, father and son, are as popular now as they were in their 19th-century heyday.

A quintessentially Viennese phenomenon, Strauss mania manifests itself in a seamless succession of concerts, exhibitions, film festivals and of course the *Fasching* (carnival) balls for which Vienna is famous. The *joie de vivre* is infectious and, if you find it just a little over the top, consider Johann Strauss the Younger, or Wild Johnny as he was known in the family – one of the greatest showmen of the age. On one occasion in 1872 he serenaded an audience of 100,000 Americans with an orchestra of no fewer than 1,000 musicians!

THE CITY

Exuberance has always been one aspect
of the Viennese character but the citizens
of this great capital have not always had
reason to celebrate. In the aftermath of
World War II, Vienna was one vast bomb
site, as depicted in the film *The Third
Man*. This was the city of shabby
intriguers, spies and foreign troops – like
Berlin, the city was divided into four
occupied sectors. Today it's very much
a part of a Europe united rather than
divided. Not that Vienna is ashamed of
its past – far from it. The marks of the
imperial capital of the Habsburgs are
evident everywhere: in the elegant
Historicist architecture of the Ring, in the
genteel and sophisticated cafés, in the
museums, concert halls and palaces.
And, while it's true that Vienna is now the
capital of a reduced and homogeneous

population compared with its polyglot past, it still has the cosmopolitan hallmarks of a world city.

Exploring Vienna is not only a joy, it couldn't be easier. One reason is its size. Despite having a population of 1.5 million, Vienna is surprisingly compact and perfect for strolling. There are a number of pedestrianized areas and most of the traffic is carried by the Ring, the stately boulevard that girdles the inner city. If you do become tired, you can resort to the fast and efficient metro system or to the distinctive red-and-white trams that rumble about town, offering visitors a cheap and entertaining sightseeing tour.

✚ 10D

ℹ Obere Augartenstrasse 40

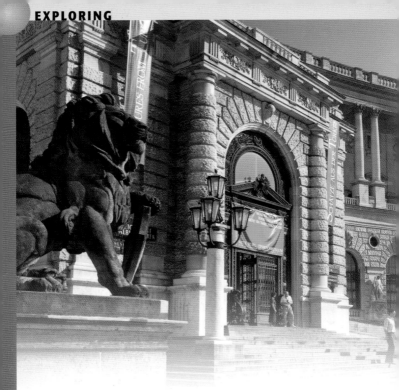

HOFBURG

The history of the Hofburg (Imperial Palace) begins in the 13th century with the building of a fortress by Rudolph I, founder of the Habsburg dynasty. However, it was not until 1619 that the palace finally became the official residence of the court. A city within a city, the vast complex of royal apartments and administrative buildings covers an area of 240,000sq m (2,583,360sq ft). There are 2,600 rooms, 19 courtyards, 18 wings and 54 main staircases. More than 5,000 people still live or work here, including the Austrian president and his officials.

The imperial apartments are open to visitors, mostly the 19th-century rooms belonging to Emperor Franz-Josef and Empress Elizabeth (Sisi). Her private suite (rooms 1–6) is the focus of the

Sisi Museum, a moving tribute to her extraordinary life and complex personality (➤ 52–53). The oldest building in the Hofburg is the 15th-century Burgkapelle (court chapel), where the Vienna Boys' Choir sings Mass on Sunday mornings (sadly, tickets are like gold dust). This is where royal marriages took place and the hearts of the Habsburgs are contained in urns in the crypt. More impressive is the white marble tomb of Archduchess Maria Christina, a masterpiece by the Italian sculptor Antonio Canova. Imperial regalia, including the 10th-century crown of Emperor Otto the Great, are on display in the Schatzkammer (Treasury). The Hofburg is best seen from Michaelerplatz – the beautifully proportioned green cupola was incorporated into Fischer von Erlach's design in the 19th century.
www.hofburg-wien.at

✚ *Wien 5d*
✉ Josefsplatz 1
☎ 01 533 7570
🕐 State Apartments: daily 9–5; Treasury: Wed–Mon 10–6; Burgkapelle: Jan–Jun, mid-Sep and Dec Mon–Thu 11–3, Fri 11–1
💰 Expensive
🚇 Herrengasse
🚌 2A, 3A

KAPUZINERGRUFT

The Kapuzinergruft is a striking testimonial to the passing of the Habsburg dynasty. In 1617 Emperor Mathias and his wife, Anna, founded the imperial tomb beneath the Kapuzinerkirche. Since then a total of 146 Habsburgs, including 12 emperors and 17 empresses, have been buried in the network of crypts and underground vaults. Many of the bronze sarcophagi are adorned with chilling *memento mori* – skeletal knights in armour, cherubs sounding the last trumpet call, cowering figures, discarded crowns and banners. The most obvious contrast is between the monumental sarcophagus, designed for Maria Theresia and her husband, Franz Stefan, and the plain tomb commissioned by their son Josef II, who detested ostentation. In 1989 Empress Zita, wife of the last Habsburg emperor, Karl I, was laid to rest in the crypt.

www.kaisergruft.at

✚ *Wien 5d* ✉ Neuer Markt, Tegetthoffstrasse ☎ 01 512 6853–12 ⏰ Daily 10–6 💰 Moderate 🚇 Stephansplatz, Karlsplatz 🚌 Hopper 3A

KUNSTHISTORISCHES MUSEUM

Best places to see, ➤ 46–47.

MUSEUMSQUARTIER

Best places to see, ➤ 54–55.

OBIZZI-PALAIS

This elegant little palace is now the home of one of the capital's more extraordinary museums: the Uhren-museum (Clock Museum), a collection of more than 3,000 timepieces dating from as early as the 15th century to

the present day. This is one of the most significant clock exhibitions in the world, and even those with no particular interest in period chronometers will find it a fascinating place to wander around. You can see water clocks, electric clocks, computerized

clocks, astronomical clocks, grandfather clocks, musical clocks, painted clocks and gilded clocks. Come at noon and you won't be able to hear yourself think for the din!

✚ *Wien 5d* ✉ Schulhof 2 ☎ 01 533 2265 🕐 Tue–Sun 9–6 ✋ Moderate 🚇 Stephansplatz, Herrengasse 🚌 Hopper 2A

ÖSTERREICHISCHES MUSEUM FÜR ANGEWANDTE KUNST

The Museum of Applied Art, often abbreviated to its initials (MAK), is one of the city's most enterprising institutions. Inspired by the Victoria and Albert Museum in London, it was founded in 1864 and moved into specially built premises, designed in a neo-Renaissance style in 1871. The collections include Italian majolica, Meissen porcelain, oriental carpets, textiles, Venetian glass, Biedermeier furniture, Judgendstil jewellery, metalwork and fashion items by leading artists of the trailblazing Wiener Werkstätte (Vienna Workshops). The museum was given a complete overhaul in 1993 when leading designers had *carte blanche* to re-create individual rooms. It's all extremely stimulating and, when you've finished, there's the MAK café, one of the best known meeting places in Vienna.

www.mak.at

✚ *Wien 6d* ✉ Stubenring 5 ☎ 01 711 36 248 🕔 Wed–Sun 10–6, Tue 10–midnight 🍴 MAK (➤ 104) ✋ Moderate 🚇 Stubentor 🚌 1, 2, 74A ❓ Tours; audio guide; special exhibitions, often avant-garde

PETERSKIRCHE

The baroque Peterskirche was completed in 1733 by Lukas Hildebrandt, better known as the architect of Schloss

Belvedere (▶ 94–95). It can't have been easy designing a building to fit into such a narrow space but the site was an important one – this is where the first Christian church stood in Roman times. Inside as well as out, the most obvious feature is the dome, though sadly the ceiling frescoes have faded so badly that they're barely visible at all from ground level. More arresting is Enzo Mattielli's monument to the martyrdom of St John Nepomuk (according to legend he was hurled into the Vltava River from the Charles Bridge in Prague). The *trompe l'oeil* effects in the choir are the work of Antonio Galli-Bibiena, famous in his day for illusionistic stage sets.

🚩 *Wien 5d* ✉ Petersplatz 1 ☎ 01 533 6433 🕐 Mon–Fri 6:30–6:30, Sat–Sun 7:30–6:30 ✋ Free 🚇 Stephansplatz 🚌 Hopper 2A

PRATER AND THE DANUBE (DONAU)

The Prater – Latin for meadow – was an imperial hunting ground long before Emperor Josef II presented it to the people of Vienna in 1766 as a 'place of entertainment'. So it's in keeping with his wishes that the main attraction of the park is the fairground, a traditional affair with bumper cars, spiral slide rides, a ghost train, slot machines, shooting ranges and a good old-fashioned merry-go-round. If the fair doesn't appeal, you can take a stroll along the 5km (3-mile) chestnut avenue known as the Hauptallee, go cycling along one of the marked paths or explore the wooded areas of the park.

To the Viennese, the Prater is synonymous with the Riesenrad, a giant Ferris wheel erected by British engineer Walter Basset in 1897. There are unbeatable views of Vienna from the wooden cabins as you climb to a maximum height of 64.7m (212ft). (The wheel turns at only 0.75m (2.5ft) a second so there's plenty of time to take photographs.)

From the Prater it's no distance at all to the River Danube. Once you've seen it, it's impossible to confuse it with the much narrower Danube Canal which skirts the inner city. The river – far from 'blue' incidentally – is artificially parted by a 21km (13-mile) strip of land called Danube Island. The best recreational facilities are at Donau Park where you can hire boats or take a cruise in summer.

✚ *Wien 8d and 7a* 🎡 Prater Funfair: Mar–Oct daily 8am–midnight; Ferris wheel: May–Sep daily 9am–midnight; closes earlier rest of year ✋ Entrance to park free; attractions (including Ferris wheel) moderate 🍴 Cafés and restaurant (€–€€) 🚇 (Park) Praterstern; (Danube) Alte Donau, Donauinsel ❓ Danube excursions: DDSG (Danube Steamship Company) ✉ Handelskai 265 ☎ 01 588 80

SCHLOSS BELVEDERE

This imposing baroque residence was built between 1714 and 1723 by the great Austrian commander Prince Eugène of Savoy. There are actually two palaces, the Unteres (Lower) and Oberes (Upper) Belvedere, connected by a sloping formal garden: Lukas Hildebrandt designed them both. After the prince's death, Schloss Belvedere was acquired by the Habsburgs. The last occupant was Archduke Franz-Ferdinand, who lived here from 1897 until his assassination in 1914.

Schloss Belvedere has several compelling art collections. In the Lower Palace you'll find an exhibition of Austrian baroque paintings and sculptures. Georg Donner's splendid fountain, copied at the Neuer Markt, is also worthy of note, as is the grimacing bust by Franz Messerschmidt in the Grotesque Room. There's a wonderful collection of medieval art in the Orangerie. The Znaim altarpiece (c1400) is a gem and there are late Gothic masterpieces by Conrad Laib and Michael Pacher.

From here it's a gentle stroll to the Upper Palace and its fabulous collection of 19th- and 20th-century paintings, including – if they're not on loan – works by Monet, Manet, Degas, Renoir and Van Gogh. There are Expressionist works by Egon Schiele and Oskar Kokoschka, while the Austrian Secessionist school is

represented by Gustav Klimt. As you leave the Belvedere, have your camera ready for the views of the Vienna skyline.
www.belvedere.at

🔀 *Wien 6e and 6f* ✉ Lower Belvedere, Orangery: Rennweg 6A; Upper Belvedere: Prinz-Eugen-Strasse 27 ☎ 01 795570 🕐 Daily 10–6. Gardens: daily 10–6 🎟 Moderate 🍴 Café/restaurant (€€) 🚉 Südbahnhof (Upper Palace) 🚌 71 (Lower Belvedere), D (Upper Belvedere), 0, 13A, 18

SCHLOSS SCHÖNBRUNN
Best places to see, ➤ 52–53.

SERVITENKIRCHE

Arguably the most appealing of Vienna's baroque churches – and one of only a few to predate the Turkish siege of 1683 – the Servitenkirche was commissioned by Prince Octavio Piccolomini in 1651, although the lavish interior was not completed for another 25 years. The architect, Carlo Canevale, was an Italian, as were the artists responsible for the magnificent stucco work. On your way out take a look at the black marble chapel of St Peregrine, patron saint of foot ailments. If the church has taken you a little out of your way, this is a quiet neighbourhood to relax in – there are tree-shaded benches in the square outside the church and a café just across the street.

✚ *Wien 5c* ✉ Servitengasse 9 ☎ 01 317 61950 🕐 8am–10pm ✋ Free
🍴 Café nearby (€–€€) 🚇 Rossauer Lände 🚋 Tram D

SEZESSION (SECESSION)

In 1897 a group of rebel artists, led by Gustav Klimt, 'seceded' from the conservative Viennese establishment to form their own association, based on the twin principles of freedom of expression and 'art for art's sake'. The Sezession building was designed for the staging of collaborative exhibitions by avant-garde artists, architects and designers with the aim of creating a *Gesamtkunst-werk* or 'total' work of art. Joseph Maria Olbrich's building outshines the Akademie der Bildenden Künste (Academy of Fine Arts) over the road. It's the dome, gilded with intertwining laurel leaves (nicknamed the 'golden cabbage' by the Viennese) that immediately strikes visitors but there are numerous other playful details – medusa heads, protruding owls, even a pair of salamanders.

✚ *Wien 5e* ✉ Friedrichstrasse 12 ☎ 01 587 5307 🕓 Tue–Sun and holidays 10–6 (Thu 10–8) 💷 Inexpensive 🚇 Karlsplatz, Oper 🚌 59A
❓ Guided tours Sat 3pm and Sun 11am

SIGMUND FREUD MUSEUM

Sigmund Freud lived and worked in this building in Vienna's 9th district from 1891 until his enforced emigration in 1938. It was here that he wrote his *Interpretation of Dreams*; here too that his patients – the subjects of the famous case histories – came for consultations and treatment. Only the waiting room is furnished as Freud left it (he took most of his belongings with him when he fled to England) but the exhibition includes home movies made in the 1930s as well as documents and photographs, labelled in English and German. You can see a few of Freud's personal possessions – his hat, coat and walking stick for example. The library too has been preserved and it contains every book published on psychoanalysis before 1938!

www.freud-museum.at

✚ *Wien 4c* ✉ Berggasse 19 ☎ 01 319 1596 🕓 Jul–Sep daily 9–6; Oct–Jun daily 9–5 💷 Moderate 🚇 Schottentor 🚌 Tram D, 37, 38, 40, 41, 42

SPANISCHE HOFREITSCHULE

The famous Spanish Riding School was designed in 1735 by Fischer von Erlach the Younger. The more prosaic title of Winter Riding School has never caught on with visitors who prefer 'Spanish', Spain being the country where the famous Lippizaner stallions originated. The training in deportment (dressage) was originally a sideline; it was their potential as cavalry horses that persuaded Archduke Karl to breed these beautiful creatures at his stud farms near Trieste.

Performances *(Vorführungen)* are held once or twice a week and last about an hour. Before 1918 the general public was excluded altogether; nowadays it's getting hold of tickets that's the problem. Each balletic routine is accompanied by music – polkas, waltzes, quadrilles, etc.

The displays of horsemanship demonstrated by the riders are as immaculate as their dress (chocolate-coloured frock coats and two-cornered hats). Among the most spectacular manoeuvres are the *Levade*, in which the horse rears up slowly, placing its entire weight on its hind quarters; the *Courbette*, where the same position is adopted before the stallion makes a series of jumps without touching the ground with its forelegs; and the *Capriole*, a leap during which the horse extends its hind and front legs.

Most performances are sold out weeks in advance, but it is easier, and cheaper, to get into a rehearsal *(Morgenarbeit)*. While there's no music, you'll be able to watch the horses and have a chance to admire the striking interior of the building.

www.srs.at

✚ *Wien 5d* ✉ Michaelerplatz 1 ☎ 01 533 9031 🕓 Performances early Feb to end Jun, Sep–Oct Sun 10:45 and some evenings. Rehearsals: Tue–Sat 10–12. Closed Jul, Aug 🚇 Herrengasse 🚌 Hopper 3A to Habsburgergasse ✋ Expensive ❓ Tickets for rehearsals sold on the day at the visitor centre (✉ Michaelerplatz 1 🕓 Tue–Sat 9–5); to reserve seats for performances write directly or book through a travel agent

STEPHANSDOM

St Stephan's Cathedral was consecrated in 1147 but only the Riesentor (Giant's Door) and the flanking 'pagan towers' remain from the various Romanesque churches. Work on the present building began early in the 14th century. The south tower, known as 'Steffl' (Little Steve), dates from 1359 and is 137m (450ft) high if you include the double-headed eagle. You can climb the 343 steps for views, or take the elevator up the north tower to see the great bell Pummerin, originally cast from abandoned Turkish cannon in 1683.

Don't miss the carved stone pulpit by Anton Pilgram (1510), a masterpiece of filigree work featuring highly individualized portraits of the Church Fathers and of the sculptor himself (seen peering from a window). Worshippers light votive candles to the miraculous Pötscher Madonna, said to have saved the city from the Turks in 1683 after shedding human tears. While you can just about see the superb Gothic vaulting of the choir from the nave, you'll get closer on the guided tour. The sublime Wiener Neustädter altar of 1447 is one of the highlights, as is the stunning red marble tomb of Frederick III.

www.stephansdom.at

✚ Wien 5d ✉ Stephansplatz

☎ 01 515 523520 🕙 Daily 6am–10pm. Guided tours Mon–Sat 10:30, 3 (Jul–Aug also 7), Sun 3. Restricted access during services.

✋ Cathedral: free. Choir tour: moderate 🚇 Stephansplatz 🚌 1A

❓ High Mass Sun 10:15am. Evening tours (including roof walk) Jun–Sep Sat 7pm

a drive in the Wienerwald (Vienna Woods)

Leave Vienna on Bundesstrasse 17, turning right at signs to Mödling.

This pretty old town was a favourite retreat of composers, including Beethoven, who wrote his *Missa Solemnis* while staying at Hauptstrasse 79.

Take Weinstrasse along the edge of vineyards to Gumpoldskirchen.

Vintners' courtyard houses line the main street of this wine-producing village. One of the best places to sample the excellent local whites is the pleasant old inn Altes Zechhaus.

Continue to the spa town of Baden (➤ 111). Leave on Bundestrasse 210.

This scenic road follows the River Schwechal through the Helenental valley, past the ruins of two medieval castles – Rauhenstein and Rauheneck – to Mayerling. It was here in 1889 that Crown Prince Rudolf committed suicide with his mistress, Maria Vetsera. The site of the hunting lodge is now marked by a neo-Gothic chapel.

Leave on route 11 to Heiligenkreuz Abbey.

The spacious abbey church, founded by the Cistercian order in 1135, is a perfect blend of Romanesque and Gothic styles. Look for the choir stalls carved with busts of the saints. Outside, the 13th-century cloisters and other buildings complete the picture of monastic life.

Continue to Gaaden, then turn northwest on the LH128, which crosses the AZ1, to Sulz im Wienerwald. After Sulz, turn right on the LH127 and continue via Kaltenleutgeben to Rodaun, then turn at the signs to 'Perchtoldsdorf Zentrum'.

The Türkenmuseum in Perchtoldsdorf town hall and the massive fortified tower in the market square are reminders of the Ottoman incursions of the 16th and 17th centuries.

Return to route 12 and continue to Vienna.

Distance 80km (50 miles)
Time 6 hours with stops, 2 without
Start/end point Vienna ✚ 10D
Lunch Altes Zechhaus (€€) ✉ Kirchenplatz 1, Gumpoldskirchen
☎ 02252 62247

HOTELS

Das Tyrol (€€–€€€)

A four-star boutique hotel on one of Vienna's chicest shopping streets, close to the MuseumsQuartier. Works of modern art in every bedroom and corridor, and an excellent breakfast.
✉ Mariahilfer Strasse 15 ☎ 01 587 5414; www.das-tyrol.at
🚇 Stephansplatz

Hotel Praterstern (€)

The plain but comfortable rooms in this pleasant hotel all have en suites.
✉ Mayergasse 6 ☎ 01 214 0123; www.hotelpraterstern.at 🚇 Praterstern

Hotel Sacher (€€€)

See page 79.

Im Palais Schwarzenberg (€€€)

See page 79.

Kärntnerhof (€€–€€€)

This quietly situated hotel, not far from St Stephen's Cathedral, has comfortable bedrooms and friendly staff.
✉ Grashofgasse 4 ☎ 01 512 1923; www.karntnerhof.com
🚇 Schwedenplatz

König von Ungarn (€€€)

This beautifully modernized hotel, virtually behind St Stephen's, is actually a 16th-century house, where Mozart once lived.
✉ Schulerstrasse 10 ☎ 01 515 840; www.kvu.at 🚇 Stephansplatz

Pension City (€€)

Friendly hotel in an elegant turn-of-the-20th-century building.
✉ Bauernmarkt 10 ☎ 01 533 9521; www.citypension.at 🚇 Stephansplatz

Pension Lerner (€€)

Plain comfortable rooms with shower and satellite TV. The hearty breakfast is a definite plus.

✉ Wipplingerstrasse 23 ☎ 01 533 5219; www.pensionlerner.com
🚇 Schottentor, Herrengasse

Pension Nossek (€€)

This ultra central guesthouse has cosy, well-appointed rooms. Just a few steps from the cathedral in a pedestrianized zone, so quiet.
✉ Graben 17 ☎ 01 533 7041-0; www.pension-nossek.at 🚇 Stephansplatz

RESTAURANTS

Bach-Hengl (€€)

The Hengl family has been associated with viticulture since 1137. This large *Heuriger* has cosy rooms, large halls and a garden.
✉ Sandgasse 7–9, Grinzing ☎ 01 320 2439 🕐 4pm–midnight

Café Central (€–€€)

This turn-of-the-20th-century café has retained its atmosphere of faded elegance. Artists and writers such as Arthur Schnitzler found their second home here.
✉ Herrengasse 14 ☎ 01 533 376-264 🚇 Herrengasse

Café Landtmann (€€)

One of Vienna's best known and stylish cafés, Landtmann is frequented by politicians, actors and other glitterati.
✉ Dr-Karl-Lueger-Ring 4 ☎ 01 241 000 🚇 Herrengasse
🕐 7:30am–midnight

Demel (€–€€)

Celebrated café with gorgeous decor, efficient service and a bewildering array of desserts. Try the *Burgtheater-Linzertorte*, shortcake flavoured with almonds and oranges.
✉ Kohlmarkt 14 ☎ 01 535 17170 🕐 Closed dinner 🚇 Herrengasse

Esterházykeller (€€–€€€)

Enjoy heart Viennese fare in these atmospheric 17th-century cellars which Joseph Haydn is said to have frequented.
✉ Haarhof ☎ 01 533 3482 🕐 Mon–Fri 11–11, Sat–Sun 4–11
🚇 Herrengasse

Figlmüller (€€€)

Figlmüller is the place to experience *schnitzel*. They reportedly serve the biggest and tastiest in town here.

✉ Bäckerstrasse 6 ☎ 01 512 1760 🕐 Noon–midnight 🚇 Stephansplatz

Frauenhuber (€€)

In the 18th century Frauenhuber was a concert hall but today it's a restaurant; slow-paced and sedate, but comfortable.

✉ Himmelpfortgasse 6 ☎ 01 512 8383 🕐 Mon–Sat 8am–midnight, Sun 10–10 🚇 Stephansplatz

Gulaschmuseum (€€)

Excellent restaurant with a good central location. The goulash dishes are well worth waiting for. Expensive wine.

✉ Schulerstrasse 20 ☎ 01 512 1017 🚇 Stephansplatz, Dr-Karl-Luger-Platz

Heiner (€€)

Stylish *patisserie* famous for its *Kouglof*, a Viennese cake.

✉ Kärntnerstrasse 21 ☎ 01 512 6863 🕐 Mon–Fri 10–6:15, Sat 10–5 🚇 Stephansplatz

Korso (€€€)

Treat yourself in one of Austria's most highly rated (and expensive) restaurants. Viennese and French cuisine at their best. Large wine list; piano accompaniment.

✉ Hotel Bristol, Kärntner Ring 1 ☎ 01 515 16546 🕐 Closed Sat lunch (and Sun lunch in Aug) 🚇 Oper, Karlsplatz 🕐 Mon–Fri 12–3, 7–11, Sat–Sun 7–11; closed Aug

Österreicher im MAK (€–€€)

Popular with young(ish) trendies, the café in the Museum of Applied Art also serves meals and is hot on vegetarian and pasta dishes. Shady courtyard for cooling off in the summer months.

✉ Stubenring 3–5 ☎ 01 714 0121 🕐 Daily 10am–1am 🚇 Stubentor

Schweizerhaus (€€)

See page 59.

Weingut Reinprecht (€€–€€€)

Typical *Heuriger* with Viennese music, home-grown wines, self-service buffet and terrace garden.

✉ Cobenzlgasse 22, Grinzing ☎ 01 320 14710 🚌 38

SHOPPING

CLOTHES AND DEPARTMENT STORES

Chegini

Fashionable women's fashions of taste and style.

✉ Kohlmarkt 7 ☎ 01 533 6091 ⏰ Mon–Fri 10–6:15, Sat 10–5

Peek & Cloppenburg

The best known (and most expensive) of several fashion stores on this busy shopping street. There are restaurants in the basement.

✉ Mariahilferstrasse 26–30 ☎ 01 525 610 ⏰ Mon–Wed 10–7, Thu–Fri 10–8, Sat 9:30–6

Naschmarkt

Source anything from Austrian football shirts and Balkan cheeses to Iranian pistachios and sauerkraut straight from the barrel at this intriguing street market. The Saturday flea market sells fasninating Viennese bric-a-brac.

✉ Wienzeile ⏰ Mon–Fri 6am–7:30pm, Sat 6–5. Flea market: Sat 6:30–4
🚇 Kettenbrückengasse

Ringstrassen Galerien

Large shopping complex in the heart of Vienna with 70 stores as well as restaurants and ample parking.

✉ Kärntner Ring 5–7, 9–13 ☎ 01 512 5181 ⏰ Mon–Fri 10–7, Sat 10–6

Trachtenmoden Shops

Outlets selling traditional clothing, including the Austrian national costume, can be found in various locations in central Vienna. Typical, and very handily situated for St Stephen's Cathedral, is Witzky.

✉ Stephansplatz 7 (near the horse and trap stop) ☎ 01 512 4843
⏰ Mon–Fri 10–6, Sat 10–4

OTHER SHOPS
Buchhandlung Tyrolia
Conveniently located just behind St Stephen's Cathedral, this large bookstore has a selection of English-language glossy titles on Vienna and Austria as well as local maps and guides.

✉ Stephansplatz 5 ☎ 01 512 4840 🕔 Mon–Fri 9–6:30, Sat 9–5

Freytag & Berndt
Detailed regional maps, guides and coffee-table books on Austria in what must be one of central Europe's largest collections.

✉ Kohlmarkt 9 ☎ 01 533 8685 🕔 Mon–Fri 9–7, Sat 9–6

Spielzeugschachtel
Large store selling a wide range of wooden and hand-crafted toys.

✉ Rauhensteingasse 5 ☎ 01 512 4494 🕔 Mon–Fri 10–6:30, Sat 10–5

ENTERTAINMENT

CLASSICAL MUSIC AND THEATRE
Bösendorfer Saal
See page 73.

Burgkapelle
This is where the Vienna Boys' Choir and members of the chorus and orchestra of the Vienna State Opera sing Mass on Sunday mornings (9:15) from Jan to late Jun and mid-Sep to Christmas. For tickets, write at least 8 weeks in advance to:

✉ Hofmusikkapelle Hofburg, Vienna A-1010 ☎ 01 533 9927; www.musikverein.at (for concert details) 🚇 Stephansdom

Burgtheater
This theatre is generally regarded as the flagship of Austrian and German drama, and the plays are in High German. It's worth visiting just for the Gustav and Ernst Klimt frescoes.

✉ Dr-Karl-Lueger-Ring 2 ☎ 01 51444 4140/4145 🚋 Tram 1, 2, to Burgtheater, Rathaus

Konzerthaus

There are three halls in this august building where you can attend classical music concerts.

✉ Lothringerstrasse 20 ☎ 01 242002 🚇 Karlsplatz

Kursalon

See page 73.

Musikverein

See page 73.

Staatsoper (State Opera)

See page 73.

Vienna's English Theatre

Mainstream drama from Britain and the US in English.

✉ Josefsgasse 12 ☎ 01 402 1260 🚇 Lerchenfelderstrasse

Volksoper

See page 73.

Wiener Kammeroper

See page 73.

NIGHTLIFE

American Bar Loos

Late-night watering hole with interior design by Secessionist artist Adolf Loos.

✉ Kärntner Durchgang (off Kärntnerstrasse 10) ☎ 01 512 3283 🕐 Sun–Thu 6pm–2am, Fri–Sat 7pm–4am 🚇 Stephansplatz

Barfly's

In the Fürst Metternich Hotel. This 6th district rhythm 'n' blues haunt is stylish. Expensive.

✉ Esterhazygasse 33 ☎ 01 586 0825 🕐 Daily 6pm–3am 🚇 Zieglergasse

Bettelstudent
The 'Hard-up Student' caters predominantly for a T-shirt-and-jeans crowd. Snacks at lunchtime and good evening pub atmosphere.
✉ Johannesgasse 12 ☎ 01 513 2044 🕐 Until late 🚇 Stadtpark

Casino Wien
See page 71.

Copa Cagrana (aka 'Sunken City')
Sprawling complex of bars, cafés, party boats and open-air discos, all with a beach theme. Fun, but keep an eye on valuables.
✉ Donauinsel, near Reichsbrücke 🕐 May–Sep, lunchtime to late

Flex
See page 71.

Jazzland
See page 71.

Krah-Krah
Busy bar in the Bermuda Triangle with snacks and an excellent choice of draught beers, and regular live music.
✉ Rabensteig 8 ☎ 01 533 8193 🕐 Mon–Sat 11am–2am, Sun and holidays 11am–1am 🚇 Schwedenplatz

Planter's Club
See page 71.

Roter Engel
The 'Red Angel' advertises itself as a 'song and wine bar'. It's stylish and there's often live music – jazz, soul, funk, you name it.
✉ Rabensteig 5 ☎ 01 535 4105 🕐 Mon–Sat 5pm–4am 🚇 Schwedenplatz

Volksgarten
Pleasant setting with an open-air dance floor in summer.
✉ Burgring 1 ☎ 01 533 0518 🕐 Sun–Thu 8pm–2am, Fri–Sat 8pm–4am
🚋 1, 2

Eastern Austria

**Eastern Austria consists of
the provinces of
Niederösterreich (Lower
Austria), Burgenland,
Steiermark (Styria) and
the Vienna basin. The
Danube valley and its
continuation, the Wachau, is wine
country and you'll see vines growing on the slopes
above the river. The scenery is idyllic and there's much
to visit: historic old towns, romantic castle ruins and
baroque churches perched on craggy promontories.**

□ Graz

Burgenland, also famous for its vineyards, was part of Hungary
until 1920 and the Magyar steppe is a characteristic feature of
the countryside. The flat terrain around the serene reed-lake,
Neusiedler See, is tailor-made for cyclists and birdwatchers. A
political football, this eastern province was for centuries in the

front line against the
marauding Turks –
hence Burgenland,
'land of castles'.

Any visit to Austria
should include the
second largest city,
Graz, a lively
university town, also
favoured by retired
people, with one of
the best preserved
old centres in
Europe. The Styrians
are an independent lot who speak their own dialect and are
fiercely proud of their homeland.

BADEN

This handsome spa town stands on the edge of the Wienerwald (Vienna Woods). For a time during the reign of Emperor Franz II (1792–1835) Baden was the official summer residence of the court, attracting dignitaries from all over Europe. It was popular with musicians: Mozart, Schubert, Brahms and the Strausses, father and son, visited, while Beethoven returned year after year.

Life here proceeds at a sedate pace. You can visit the thermal baths or take a stroll through the elegant streets to enjoy the 19th-century Biedermeier architecture. When you're through with sightseeing, head for the beautiful surroundings of the Kurpark where there's a casino and an outdoor concert theatre.

🕂 10D 🔼 Baden ❓ Kurpark concerts: Jun–early Sep Thu–Sun 4:30
ℹ️ Brusattiplatz, Leopoldsbad ☎ 02252 22600-600

BRUCK AN DER LEITHA

The River Leitha once marked the border between Austria and Hungary. Bruck itself is a pleasant, easy-going town and a convenient stopover if you're thinking of visiting Haydn's birthplace at Rohrau. From the baroque Hauptplatz it's a short walk to the attractive 18th-century parish church (Pfarrkirche). The castle was rebuilt in English Tudor style for the Harrach family in the 1850s and looks slightly the worse for wear. It's not open to the public but there's a nice ivy-clad restaurant with a shady courtyard on the edge of the grounds. From Bruck it's a short drive to Bruckneudorf and the extensive ruins of a 34-room **Roman villa** begun in the reign of the Emperor Hadrian (2nd century AD).

🕂 11D ✉️ 40km (25 miles) southeast of Vienna
ℹ️ Hauptplatz ☎ 02162 62221

Roman Villa (Kaiservilla)

✉️ Bruckneudorf ☎ 02162 62264 🕒 Guided tours Jun–Sep 🖐️ Moderate

DÜRNSTEIN

Best places to see, ➤ 36–37.

EISENSTADT

This unassuming town is famous both for its wine and for its associations with the composer Joseph Haydn. Born in nearby Rohrau in 1732, Haydn entered the service of the Esterházy family in 1761 and remained with them for more than 40 years. Haydn's patron, Prince Nikolaus Esterházy, created a lavish and ostentatious court which, culturally at least, rivalled Vienna.

Schloss Esterházy is the imposing baroque residence built for the family in the late 17th century (the towers allude to the medieval fortress which once occupied the site). Visitors are only allowed into the apartments on a guided tour conducted in German, but you can enjoy the frescoed ceiling and opulent surroundings of the 18th-century concert hall, the Haydnsaal, by attending one of the weekly concerts. Tours of the wine cellars are also available.

The modest house in which Haydn lived from 1766 to 1788 and where he kept chickens and a couple of horses is now a **museum.** There's little in the way of period atmosphere, although you can see instruments played by members of the Esterházy orchestra and one of Haydn's organs.

Haydn's mortal remains now lie in the bloated baroque **Bergkirche,** where he regularly played the organ and where many of his masses were first performed. Completed in 1722, the church's main attraction is the extraordinary Kalvarienberg, whose cross consists of 24 tableaux and more than 300 painted statues. There are great views of the countryside from the top.

➕ 11E ✉ 45km (28 miles) south of Vienna
ℹ Schloss Esterházy ☎ 02682 63384/800 847 26837

Schloss Esterházy
✉ Esterházy Platz ☎ 02682 719 3220 🕐 Apr–Oct daily 8:30–6; Nov–Mar, Mon–Fri 9–5 ✋ Moderate ❓ Concerts in Haydnsaal every weekend May–Oct; Haydntage festival Sep

Haydnmuseum
✉ Joseph-Haydn-Gasse 21 ☎ 02682 62652 29 🕐 Apr–Oct daily 9–5 ✋ Moderate

Bergkirche
✉ Haydnplatz 1 ☎ 02682 62638 🕐 Apr–Oct daily 9–12, 1–5 ✋ Moderate

GRAZ

Austria's second largest city, Graz rivalled Vienna in importance until Ferdinand II moved his court to the capital early in the 17th century. The superb skyline of palatial Renaissance and baroque residences is very impressive, but Graz offers a great deal more than architecture. Apart from a host of musical and theatrical events, culminating in the contemporary international arts festival, Steirische Herbst (Styrian Autumn), Graz has its own 'Bermuda Triangle' of bars and restaurants, fuelled by a student population in excess of 40,000. Graz was European Cultural Capital in 2003.

The Schlossberg is Graz's most obvious landmark. The castle was demolished in 1809 on the orders of Napoleon, leaving only the casemates and a couple of towers intact. The Kriegssteig, a flight of 260 stone steps, zigzags up the hill to the Uhrturm (clock tower) or you can take the funicular. Look closely and you'll see that the hands on the brightly painted clockface have been swapped round.

The Herberstein Gardens below have been planted with lemon and fig trees, pomegranate shrubs and wisterias. Look out over the terrace for panoramic views of the city. Near the top of the hill

is the Glockenturm (bell tower). The bell, known as 'Lisl', was cast from 101 Turkish cannon balls.

The magnificent Landhaus was designed in 1557 by Domenico dell'Allio for the Styrian parliament. Look into the arcaded courtyard before going next door to the former Arsenal, the **Landeszeughaus** (note the martial statues of Mars and Bellona on either side of the doorway). Preserved almost exactly as it was in the 1640s, it has a staggering 30,000 exhibits: swords, muskets, crossbows, suits of armour (including a full set of horse armour), cannons, powder horns and chain mail. For more than two centuries (1471–1689), Graz played a crucial role in the defence of Europe against the Turks. It was here that members of the Styrian army were fitted out before being marched to the front. The Landeszeughaus is also a splendid architectural monument, best appreciated from the top of the building where there's a superb view across the courtyard towards the Schlossberg.

The 15th-century **Domkirche** (cathedral) has retained much of its original Gothic appearance. A faded medieval fresco on the south wall depicts the Turks as a scourge equal to the plague itself, while inside there's a 15th-century crucifixion by Konrad Laib. The extraordinary domed building alongside the cathedral is the mausoleum of Ferdinand II, designed by Pietro de Pomis in 1614. Ferdinand's tomb is to the right of the altar.

Schloss Eggenberg was the imposing baroque palace of one of Austria's most distinguished families. Also designed by Pietro de Pomis, it represents an

elaborate allegory of universal order: four towers standing for the points on the compass, 365 windows for the days of the year, 24 state apartments for the hours of the day and so on. Peacocks preen themselves in the landscaped park where deer also roam. The most impressive of the Prunkräume (State Apartments) is the Planetensaal (Planet Hall) with paintings by Styrian artist Hans Weissenkircher.

www.graztourismus.at

✚ 22J ✉ 140km (87 miles) southwest of Vienna 🚆 Graz ✈ Internal flights
❓ Tours of Schlossberg and old town (ask at tourist information office); Styriarte (Jun, Jul); Steirischer Herbst (Oct)
ℹ Herrengasse 16 ☎ 0316 80750

Landeszeughaus

✉ Herrengasse 16 ☎ 0316 8017 9810; www.zeughaus.at ⏰ Apr–Oct daily 10–6; Nov–Mar Mon–Sat 10–5, Sun 10–4 ✋ Moderate

a walk around Graz

From Hauptplatz turn into Sackstrasse, lined with former residences of the Austrian nobility.

Palais Khuenburg (No 18) was the birthplace of Archduke Franz-Ferdinand in 1863. The rococo Palais Herberstein (No 16, open to the public) belonged to the Eggenberg family, while the Counts of Attems lived in the baroque mansion opposite (No 17).

At Schlossbergplatz climb the terraces to the Schlossberg (➤ 115). Leave the hill via Sporgasse.

This narrow shopping street also contains some fine historic houses – for example, the Renaissance 'Zur Goldenen Pastete' (No 28) and the Palais Saurau (No 25) – note the carved figure of a Turkish warrior under the cornice.

Turn left into Hofgasse, passing the court bakery, the theatre and the town castle.

The castle boasts an impressive double spiral staircase (1499) – look under the arch in the first courtyard.

Cross to the Domkirche (► 116), then take the steps between the cathedral and mausoleum to Bürgergasse. From here Abraham-St Clara Gasse leads to Glockenspielplatz.

The celebrated Glockenspiel (musical clock) entertains the crowds three times a day (11am, 3pm and 6pm).

Take Engegasse, then Stempfergasse to Herrengasse. Cross to the Landeszeughaus (► 116). Follow Landhausgasse past the heraldic arms of the old Styrian cities on the walls of the Landhaus. Turn right into Schmiedgasse and continue to Hauptplatz.

The busy heart of Graz was first laid out in 1164 and still has its daily market. The most eye-catching of the façades surrounding the town hall is the Luegghaus (corner of Sporgasse).

Distance 3km (2 miles)
Time 2–4 hours depending on visits
Start/end point Hauptplatz
Lunch Café Glockenspiel
✉ Glockenspielplatz 4
☎ 0664 2428 893

KREMS AN DER DONAU

There are actually three communities here: Krems itself, Und and Stein. Once the seat of the Babenberg dukes, Krems has preserved a good deal of its architectural heritage, including the Steiner Tor (a monumental gateway and local landmark), the Renaissance town hall dating from 1491 and medieval burghers' houses in Landstrasse. As you explore the cobbled streets of the

old centre look for lively paintings of revellers on the façade of the Sgraffitohaus and the loggia of the Palais Gozzo in Hoher Markt. The local history museum (Weinstadtmuseum), housed in a former Dominican monastery, has exhibitions on the wine-making industry and other trades, and you can also visit the original 13th-century chapel and cloisters. A prolific 18th-century artist, Johann 'Kremser' Schmidt, decorated the ceiling of the dramatically baroque parish church of St Veit. Schmidt was also responsible for the frescoes in the church of St Nikolaus in Stein (see below) and the altarpiece in the Gothic Piaristenkirche (Church of the Order of Piarists).

The tourist office in the former Capuchin monastery in Und has an exhibition on the history of wine-making, although Und is better known for *Bailoni*, an apricot liqueur – many houses are decorated with fruit motifs. Surprisingly few visitors get as far as Stein, despite its charms, which include wonderful Renaissance façades, two picturesque salt barns and a former bishop's residence decorated with towers and crenellations. Art exhibitions are held in the 13th-century Minoritenkirche, now partly restored.

www.krems.info

✚ 9C ✉ 60km (37 miles) west of Vienna
🚉 Krems 🚢 Brandner Schiffahrt (✉ Ufer 50, Wallsee ☎ 07433 259021) runs Danube cruises between Melk, Dürnstein and Krems
ℹ Undstrasse 6 ☎ 02732 82676

MARIAZELL

Famous as a place of pilgrimage, the **basilica** of Mariazell was founded by the Benedictines in 1157, but the shrine didn't acquire cult status until Louis I of Hungary attributed his victory over the Turks to the intervention of the Virgin of Mariazell in 1377. For believers, the focal point is the 12th-century statue of the Virgin, displayed behind a silver grille in the Gnadenkapelle (Miracles Chapel). The gorgeous high altar, by the great baroque master Fischer

von Erlach the Elder, was commissioned by Emperor Charles VI. In the Schatzkammer (treasury) the ex-votos, dating back to medieval times, bear witness to the power of faith.

The world's oldest steam tramway runs (summer weekends only) between Mariazell and the Erlaufsee lake. For walks and wonderful views of the Hochschwab mountains, take the **cable-car** to the Bürgeralpe. Alternatively, drive to Hieflau, following the Salza ravine through forested and increasingly wild countryside.

🔢 8E ✉ 80km (50 miles) north of Graz 🚌 Dr-Leber-Strasse (centre). Services from Bruck and Graz 🚆 Mariazell-St Sebastian (15 minutes) 🛈 Hauptplatz 13 ☎ 03882 2366

Basilica

✉ Kardinal-Eugen-Tisserant-platz 1 ☎ 03882 2595 🕐 Daily; Schatzkammer: May–Oct Tue–Sat 10–3 and weekends 11–3 ❓ Main events at the basilica are on major Marian feasts (15 Aug, 8 Sep) and at Whitsun

Cable-car to Bürgeralpe

☎ 03882 2555 🕐 Dec–Apr daily 9–4; May–Oct 9–5 ✋ Moderate

MELK

See pages 50–51.

MURTAL

One of the best ways to see the hilly, densely wooded Mur valley is to ride on the narrow-gauge railway that operates between Tamsweg in the Salzburger Land and Unzmarkt, west of Judenburg. The same company operates steam services in the summer with tourists in mind (trains connect Murau to Tamsweg or Stadl). Murau itself is a lovely town. It was founded by Ulrich of Liechtenstein, who built a castle here in the 13th century. Much of the town's medieval defences has survived, including parts of the old walls and the fortified town hall. The parish church dates from 1296 and contains some remarkable frescoes. Schloss Obermurau (rebuilt in the 17th century) looms over the fast-flowing river and the town, with its winding streets and timbered houses.

🔢 19J ✉ 60km (37 miles) northwest of Graz 🚆 Murtalbahn 🕐 Daily; steam train Tue, Jun to mid-Sep (and Sat in Aug) 🛈 Budesstrasse 13A, Murau ☎ 03532 27200

NEUSIEDLER SEE/SEEWINKEL NATIONALPARK

This serene steppe lake, covering an area of about 320sq km (123sq miles), is the largest in Europe. Surrounded by vineyards and grassy plains, the screen of tall reedbeds is so dense in places that it's difficult to make out the water at all. Much of the region is now a national park, administered jointly by Austria and Hungary. While fully geared to tourism, environmental protection measures have ensured that Neusiedler See is not in any way spoiled. There's a host of activities available, from swimming (the warm brackish water is nowhere more than about 2m/6ft deep) to sailing, windsurfing, hiking, tennis and golf. Cycling is especially encouraged: there are 1,000km (620 miles) of signposted tracks with rental and repair shops in most villages.

If you're planning on staying in the area, give Neusiedl am See a wide berth in favour of Rust or Purbach. Rust is lively as well as pretty, the façades of its baroque and Renaissance houses painted in soft pastel colours. The main sight is the Fischerkirche, founded in the 12th century and enclosed within a protective wall to defend it against the Turks. The frescoes inside date back to the 14th century.

Purbach is a little more off the beaten track. Delightfully unpretentious, it boasts an entire street lined with grass-covered wine cellars, as well as many historic winegrowers' houses. At one time the Turks were almost permanently encamped outside the village. Parts of the defensive walls have survived, along with the Türkentor, a double gateway built between 1630 and 1634.

Purbach's most celebrated resident was the legendary 'Purbacher Turk': left behind by the retreating Ottoman army after getting drunk, he converted to Christianity and prospered.

Mörbisch is equally picturesque. You'll enjoy the Hofgassen (alleyways running off the main streets) where the houses are decorated with flowers and the traditional bunches of grain. Mörbisch is best known for the Seefestspiele, an operetta festival held on the largest floating stage in Europe.

✚ 11E ✉ 40km (25 miles) southeast of Vienna ☎ National Park: 02175 3442 🚉 Neusiedl am See, Purbach, Frauenkirchen ⛴ Mörbisch-Illmitz May–Oct 8:30–5 every 30 minutes ❓ Seefestspiele, Mörbisch: tickets from Eisenstadt ☎ 02682 66210; www.seefestspiele-moerbisch.at
ℹ Schloss Esterházy, Eisenstadt ☎ 02682 63384; Hauptgasse 38, Purbach ☎ 02683 5920; Conradplatz 1, Rust ☎ 02685 502

a drive through the Weinviertel (Wine District)

Take Bundestrasse 7 north from Vienna to Poysdorf.

This town at the heart of the Weinviertel has been producing wine since the 14th century. It's a good place to see *Kellergassen* – rows of turf-covered wine cellars, usually on the edge of town. Some open their doors to prospective buyers who can sample the wines at a table in the *Presshaus* (cellar).

Take the 219 to Staatz, then turn right on route 46 to Laa an der Thaya.

Right on the border with the Czech Republic, Laa is not a town to linger in unless you're interested in beer – the Hubertus brewery has been supplying local inns since 1454. If you happen to be around in mid-September, take a look at the colourful Onion Festival.

Take the 45 through Hadres to Haugsdorf. Continue to the junction with route 30, then turn right to Retz.

Retz's windmill, set among vineyards at the edge of the town, is the local landmark. It's also famous for the red wines produced by the Weinbauschule. Beneath the picturesque town square is Austria's largest network of cellars, dating from the 15th century. Tours are organized from the Rathaus.

Leave Retz on route 35 to Eggenburg.

This ancient town has well-preserved walls, a church dating from the 12th century and a pillory in the Hauptplatz. For motorcycle enthusiasts, the **Österreichisches Motorradmuseum** (Museumgasse 6), with over 300 makes of bikes displayed in a former factory, is a must.

Return to Vienna on Bundestrasse 303, turning off on to route 3 at Stockerau to avoid the Autobahn.

Distance 200km (124 miles)
Time 9 hours (5 hours without stops)
Start/end point Vienna ✚ 10D
Lunch Schlossgasthaus Brand (€€) ✉ Schlossplatz 5, Retz
☎ 02942 2494 ⊕ Closed Mon

WALDVIERTEL

The castles and monasteries of the region are best explored by car – Krems an der Donau (▶ 120–121) makes a good touring base. The glorious Benedictine **Stift Altenburg** (abbey), with its lavishly decorated apartments and ceiling frescoes by Paul Troger, rates as the top attraction, followed by the romantic Cistercian monastery **Stift Zwettl.** The pick of the castles must be **Heidenreichstein,** a moated fortress with ramparts that have never been scaled by attackers. Also consider Schloss Hardegg and Rosenau, a rococo castle boasting Europe's only museum of freemasonry.

➕ 8C ✉ 50km (31 miles) northwest of Vienna

Stift Altenburg
🕐 Easter–1 Nov daily 10–5 ✋ Moderate

Stift Zwettl
🕐 May–Oct Mon–Sat tour 10, 11, 2, 3, Sun 11, 2, 3 (also 4 Jul–Sep) ✋ Moderate

Heidenreichstein
🕐 Mid-Apr to mid-Oct Tue–Sun 9, 10, 11, 2, 3, 4 ✋ Moderate

HOTELS

BADEN
Grand Hotel Sauerhof (€€€)
Stylish, luxury hotel in a former palace. Facilities include indoor swimming pool, sauna and tennis court.
✉ Weilburgstrasse 11–13 ☎ 02252 412510; www.sauerhof.at

DÜRNSTEIN
Hotel Schloss Dürnstein (€€€)
See page 78.

EISENSTADT
Gasthof Familie Ohr (€)
Quiet, comfortable rooms and an excellent restaurant (closed Mon) are the main attractions of this medium-sized hotel.
✉ Rusterstrasse 51 ☎ 02682 62460; www.hotelohr.at

Hotel Burgenland (€€)
Modern hotel short on character but with the perfect location, just across the road from Schloss Esterhazy. Swimming pool.
✉ Franz-Schubert Platz 1 ☎ 02682 6960; www.hotelburgenland.at

GRAZ
Hotel Drei Raben (€€)
Modern hotel on a busy street with tram routes. Comfortable and surprisingly quiet given the location.
✉ Annenstrasse 43 ☎ 0316 712686; www.dreiraben.at

Hotel Schlossberg (€€€)
See page 78.

KREMS
Gästehaus Einzinger (€)
Centred around a 16th-century courtyard filled with potted plants and bird cages. Rooms vary from period to modern.
✉ Steiner Landstrasse 82, Stein ☎ 02732 82316;
www.gaesthaus-einzinger.at

NEUSIEDLER SEE
Romantik-Purbachhof (€€)
See page 79.

Rusterhof (€€€)
Former Burgherhaus in the centre of this delightful little town with rooms and apartments. The restaurant is also worth investigating.

✉ Rathausplatz 18, Rust ☎ 02685 6416; www.tiscover.at/rusterhof
🕓 Closed Jan to mid-Mar

RESTAURANTS

BADEN
Krainerhütte (€€)
This well-appointed restaurant is in a 19th-century country-style hotel on the edge of town. International and Austrian cooking.

✉ Helenental ☎ 02252 445110

Rauhenstein (€€–€€€)
Located in Sauerhof Hotel this restaurant has the best dining in town in an atmospheric arched dining room. Jazz brunches.

✉ Weilburgstrasse 11 ☎ 02252 412510

BRUCK AN DER LEITHA
Ungarische Krone (€€–€€€)
The 'Hungarian Crown' is a country-style inn, founded in 1726. Excellent cooking and first-class wines.

✉ Parndorfer Strasse 1 ☎ 02162 62777

DÜRNSTEIN
Weinschenke Altes Presshaus (€)
Wash down sausages, cold meat platters and sandwiches with local Grüner Veltliner and other Wachau vintages at this old-fashioned wine cellar. Choose between the whitewashed interior with its tree-trunk ceiling, or the outside seating with views of the castle.

✉ Düenstein 10 ☎ 0699 1196 6252 🕓 Tue–Sun 10am–11pm

EISENSTADT

Café Esterházy (€€)

Located in the former stables of the castle, this chic eatery caters mainly for the theatre supper set. The bar stays open late, a point well worth remembering in this otherwise quiet town.

✉ Esterházyplatz 5 ☎ 02682 62819

Haydnbräu (€€)

Modern restaurant serving a typical range of Austrian dishes including fish, as well as excellent local beer.

✉ Pfarrgasse 22 ☎ 02682 63945

GRAZ

Der Steirer (€€)

Styrian cuisine minus the *lederhosen* and oompah bands. Enjoy traditional dishes in a 21st-century setting, then head next door to the speciality food shop to buy ingredients and wine to take home.

✉ Belgiergasse 1 ☎ 0316 703654 🕘 Daily 11am–midnight

Glockenspiel (€)

An ideal place to stop for a coffee and a sandwich (or pastry) while waiting for the musical clock to go through its paces

✉ Glockenspielplatz 4 ☎ 0644 2428893

Landhauskeller (€€€)

See page 58.

Mangolds (€)

Self-service vegetarian restaurant with a good selection of healthy dishes. No credit cards.

✉ Griesgasse 11 ☎ 0316 718002 🕘 Mon–Fri 11–7, Sat 10–4; closed Sat Jul–Aug

Schlossberg (€)

Terrace café with panoramic views of the city. The speciality of the house is *Germknödeln* (poppy seed dumplings).

✉ Schlossberg 7 ☎ 0316 840000

KREMS AN DER DONAU
Alte Post (€–€€)
Appealing house, with a delightful Renaissance courtyard, located in the centre of Krems. Traditional Austrian dishes. No credit cards.

✉ Obere Landstrasse 32 ☎ 02732 82276 🕐 Closed Jan–beginning of Apr, also Tue–Wed

Jell (€€)
See page 58.

MARIAZELL
Gasthof zum Jägerwirt (€€)
Schnitzels, goulash dishes and other Austrian standards; also snacks and salads. No credit cards.

✉ Hauptplatz 2 ☎ 03882 2362 🕐 Closed Mon

Ochsenwirt (€€)
Popular family restaurant with grill specialities and friendly atmosphere. Terrace seating available in summer.

✉ A. Krupp-Platz 3 ☎ 03882 2407 🕐 Closed Tue

Zum alten Brauhaus (€)
Styrian specialities washed down, ideally, by the excellent local Girrer brew, available on tap (ask for *Bier vom Fass*).

✉ Wienerstrasse 5 ☎ 03882 25230

NEUSIEDLER SEE
Martinschenke (€€)
A folksy thatched restaurant and grillhouse with garden and candlelit interior. Serves standard Austrian fare with fresh salads and a good selection of local wines.

✉ Bodenzeile 14–16, Purbach ☎ 02683 5151 🕐 Closed Wed

Nikolauszeche (€€€)
Dining in this top-notch village restaurant will set you back a bit, but it's worth it both for the setting in a 15th-century house and

for the superb regional cuisine. The more exotic specialities include pink fillet of young goat and the wines are from the Nikolauszeche cellars.

✉ Bodenzeile 3, Purbach ☎ 02683 5514 🕒 Closed Wed Mar–Nov

Schandl (€–€€)
Plain home cooking is what's on offer in this typical Neusiedler See inn (*Buschenschank*). There's an attractive courtyard and the wines are good too. No credit cards.

✉ Hauptstrasse 20, Rust ☎ 02685 265 🕒 Closed Tue and Nov–Mar

Seewirt (€€)
The restaurant in this waterfront hotel is good for local dishes, including fish.

✉ Strandplatz 1, Podersdorf ☎ 02177 2415 🕒 Closed Dec–Jan

SHOPPING

DEPARTMENT STORE
Kastner & Öhler
Huge glass-fronted department store selling everything from children's toys to Austrian folk music, CDs and videos, clothes etc.

✉ Sackstrasse 7–13, Graz ☎ 0316 8700 🕒 Mon–Fri 9:30–7, Sat 9:30–6

OTHER SHOPS
Eugen Bailoni
Few can resist the temptation to take home a couple of bottles of fine schnapps made from local apricots by this Krems company. The factory shop in Stein has by far the biggest range of products.

✉ Steiner Landstrasse 100–102, Krems an der Donau ☎ 02732 82228
🕒 Mon–Thu 7–12, 1–5, Fri 7–12

Steirisches Heimatwerk
See page 62.

Vitrine
Splendid selection of art deco and 19th-century jewellery, glassware, figurines, curios, vases, pewter, bronze, silverware and

much more in this delightful antique shop almost at the foot of the castle steps.

✉ Sackstrasse 15 ☎ 0664 1014751 ◑ Mon–Fri 10–12:30, 3–6, Sat 10–12:30

ENTERTAINMENT

CLASSICAL MUSIC AND THEATRE

For information and ticket reservations for Graz's two major festivals, Styriarte and Steirischer Herbst (Styrian Autumn), write to the address below. Styriarte takes place from late June to mid-July and attracts international classical musicians as well as local Nikolaus Harnoncourt and his various orchestras. Styrian Autumn is an avant-garde festival of theatre, music, dance, jazz and film.

✉ Palais Attems, Sackstrasse 17, A-8010, Graz ☎ Steirischer Herbst: 0316 816070; Styriarte: 0316 825000 or tickets@styriate.com

Opera Haus (Opera House)
See page 72.

NIGHTLIFE
Café Harrach
Student pub near the university with a relaxed atmosphere.

✉ Harrachgasse 26, Graz ☎ 0316 322671 ◑ Mon–Fri 9am–midnight, from 6pm summer

Casino Graz
See page 70.

Miles Jazz Bar
See page 70.

M1
Striking blue glass building by architect Richard Ellmer. The bars are on the upper floors, with fine views of the city.

✉ Färberplatz 1, Graz ☎ 0316 811233 ◑ Mon–Sat 9pm–2am

Central Austria

The central part of Austria includes Oberösterreich (Upper Austria), Kärnten (Carinthia), part of Steiermark (Styria) and most of Salzburger Land. Salzburg, regarded by many as one of the world's most beautiful cities, is, of course, synonymous with Mozart and the Salzburg Festival. Italianate in appearance, it's stolidly Germanic in character and conservative by nature.

Salzburg

To the east is Austria's stunning lake district, the Salzkammergut – *salz* (salt) being the source of its wealth since prehistoric times. The brine spa at Bad Ischl became fashionable in the 19th century after Emperor Franz-Josef established his summer residence here.

Mahler, like Brahms, was inspired by the Carinthian lakes – don't be put off by the far-fetched misnomer 'Austrian Riviera', usually applied to the Wörther See, but only really true of Velden – the rest is quite unspoiled.

SALZBURG

One of Europe's most beautiful – and most conservative – cities, Salzburg spreads out along the banks of the Salzach River with the lower Alps beyond. Until 1816 Salzburg was an independent city state, ruled by prince-archbishops from the brooding Hohensalzburg fortress. One of them, Hieronymous von Colloredo, was the patron of Mozart, who was born here in 1756. Every year the Salzburg Festival (➤ 164) honours the composer in a feast of opera, orchestral music and theatre.

✚ 3E ✉ 225km (140 miles) west of Vienna 🚆 Salzburg
✈ International flights
ℹ 5 Mozartplatz ☎ 0662 88987330; www.salzburg.info

Domkirche

When Salzburg's Romanesque basilica burned down in 1598, Archbishop Wolf Dietrich resolved to build a cathedral to rival St Peter's in Rome. His successor was less ambitious; even so, this magnificent church, designed by Italian architect Santino Solari and not completed until 1655, is one of the finest early baroque monuments north of the Alps. The beautifully proportioned façade, constructed from pink Untersberg marble, is matched by the spacious interior, crowned by an immense cupola. Mozart was baptized in the 12th-century font (note the four copper lions guarding the base); the composer would also have recognized the organ which dates from 1702 to 1703.

✉ Domplatz ☎ 0662 8047 1870 🕓 Dommuseum (treasury) mid-May to mid-Oct Mon–Sat 10–5, Sun 11–6 ✋ Donation ❓ Sung Mass Sun 10am; organ recitals Jul–Sep

Franziskanerkirche

The Romanesque nave of the Franciscan church was adapted to harmonize with the lofty Gothic chancel, a forest of slender granite columns crowned by vaults added in the 15th century. The elaborate baroque altar, designed by Fischer von Erlach, contains a medieval madonna by the Tirolean sculptor Michael Pacher.

✉ Franziskanergasse 5 🕐 Summer: daily 6:30am–8pm (to 6pm winter)

Hohensalzburg

Founded in 1077, the fortress was substantially enlarged in the 16th century. There are panoramic views from the terrace near the Kuenburg Bastion (c1680). In the main courtyard look for the cistern, dating from 1539, which stands beneath a lime tree nearly 350 years old. To visit the interior you'll need to sign up for the 40-minute guided tour. The State Apartments are the main attraction, notably the Golden Chamber, sumptuously decorated with gilded woodcarving and a gorgeous majolica stove. You also see the torture chamber, the prison cells and the hand-driven mechanical organ known as the Salzburg Steer (1502), for which Mozart's father composed chorales.

Five minutes' walk from the foot of the castle is the oldest convent in central Europe. **Stift Nonnberg** was founded in the 8th century and is a 'must see' for *Sound of Music* fans – it was here that Maria von Trapp tried her vocation as well as the patience of her Mother Superior! Inside there's a beautiful Gothic altar and medieval frescoes of St Rupert and Pope Gregory the Great.

✉ Mönchsberg 34, 120m (393ft) above town ☎ 0662 84243011 🕐 Jan–Apr, Oct–Dec daily 9:30–5; May–Jun, Sep daily 9–6; Jul–Aug daily 9–7
🍴 Restaurant (€€) 🖐 Moderate 🚠 Funicular: Jan–Apr, Oct–Dec daily 9–5; May–Sep daily 9–9 (every 10 minutes) ❓ Concerts (ask at tourist information)

Stift Nonnberg

☎ 0662 841 607 🕐 Autumn, spring daily 7–12, 1:30–5; summer till 7:30

Mozarts Geburtsh

Mozarts Geburtshaus

It was on the third floor of this elegant apartment building that Salzburg's most famous son was born on 27 January, 1756. While the museum is disappointingly short on atmosphere (only one of the rooms has been furnished as a 'typical bourgeois interior'), the personal effects, especially

the miniature violin Mozart learnt to play as a child, have a particular fascination. As well as a lock of the composer's hair, his silk purse, tobacco case and ring, you can see an array of portraits, autograph letters and scores. The view across the courtyard towards the Kollegienkirche can't have changed much since Mozart's day.

✉ Getreidegasse 9 ☎ 0662 844313
🕐 Sep–Jun daily 9–6; Jul–Aug daily 9–7
✋ Moderate (combined ticket with Wohnhaus available) 🍴 Café Trzesniewski (ground floor) (€)

Mozart-Wohnhaus

The eight-room apartment the Mozart family rented from 1773 to 1780 contains a fascinating exhibition which places the composer's life in context. Just pick up a headset and wander through the rooms, listening to the commentary which adjusts automatically. There are entertaining details concerning the Mozarts' domestic situation and of course their musical activities. The exhibits include the pianoforte Mozart used for concerts and more domestic items such as a tea and sugar box. Most of his early life was spent touring Europe; an interactive video charts each of the main journeys and you can read what he thought of his fellow musicians by perusing the autograph letters.

✉ Makartplatz 8 ☎ 0662 874227 🕐 Sep–Jun daily 9–6; Jul–Aug daily 9–7
✋ Moderate (combined ticket with Geburtshaus available)

Peterskirche

This 12th-century Romanesque basilica was given a thorough rococo face-lift in the 1770s when the original wooden ceiling was replaced by baroque vaulting and the frescoes were whitewashed to make way for paintings by Caspar Memberger, Antonio Solari and others. The fabulous organ featured in the première of Mozart's C minor mass in 1783.

The churchyard is Salzburg's oldest (1627). Pressed against the hillside are the chapels, crypts and mausoleums of Salzburg's most illustrious families; Mozart's sister and Haydn's brother are also buried here. You can also visit the catacombs, a network of caves used as a cemetery by Christians in the 3rd century AD.

✉ St Peter Bezirk 🕐 Varies. Check in advance. Catacombs: May–Sep daily 10–5; Oct–Apr daily 10:30–3:30 (short guided tours on the hour) 💷 Free (catacombs inexpensive)

Residenz

Looking out on to the Residenzplatz is the palace of the Archbishop of Salzburg, founded in the 12th century and rebuilt between 1595 and 1619. The sumptuous State Apartments can be visited on a 50-minute guided tour which includes the Conference Hall where Mozart conducted the court orchestra. The Residenzgalerie houses the princely art collection, strong on 17th-century Dutch and Flemish painting. The most famous works are Rembrandt's *Old Woman Praying* and Rubens' *Allegory of Charles V as Master of the World*.

✉ Residenzplatz 1 ☎ 0662 840451 🕐 State Apartments: daily 10–5. Residenzgalerie: Tue–Sun 10–5 💷 Moderate

Schloss Hellbrunn

This early baroque country estate was built for Prince-archbishop Markus Sittikus von Hohenems between 1613 and 1619 by Santino Solari. Trick fountains, grottoes, fish ponds and a mechanical theatre operated by water are among the attractions of

the beautiful landscaped gardens. There's also a folklore museum and a theatre but, if you have children with you, you might skip these in favour of the zoo. The more unusual animals include the alpine ibex, the snow leopard and the red panda, and there's a special area where children can pet the animals.

✉ Fürstenweg 37 (5km/3 miles south of town) ☎ 0662 820372

🕐 Hellbrunn: Mar–Apr, Oct daily 9–4:30; May–Jun, Sep daily 9–5:30; Jul–Aug daily 9am–10pm

✋ Expensive 🍴 Café (€€) 🚌 25 from train station or Rathaus

❓ Guided tours of Schloss/fountains

a walk around Salzburg

The gardens of Schloss Mirabell were laid out in 1690 by Fischer von Erlach. They can best be appreciated from the terrace at the top of the steps where Julie Andrews and the Von Trapp children performed the *Do-Re-Mi* song in *The Sound of Music*.

Walk down Schwarzstrasse, past the Mozart-Wohnhaus (▶ 141) to Staatsbrücke. Cross the River Salzach into Rathausplatz. Turn left on to Judengasse. Follow the road to the Waagplatz, then pass under the arch by St Michael's church into Residenzplatz.

In the centre of the square is the 18th-century column to the Virgin Mary. Opposite the Residenz (➤ 142) is the Glockenspiel – performances daily at 11am and 6pm.

Cross Domplatz in front of the cathedral (➤ 136), then go through the arch into Kapitelplatz, where chess players challenge each other on a giant-sized board. At the top of the square you'll find the cable-car to Hohensalzburg (➤ 138). Walk through the cemetery of Peterskirche (➤ 142). From the church, cross the courtyard and turn left on to Franziskanergasse.

Opposite the Franziskanerkirche (➤ 138) is the Rupertinum, a gallery of 20th-century art with a handful of paintings by Klimt and his contemporaries Kokoschka, Nolde and Kirchner.

Continue on Franziskanergasse to Max-Reinhardtplatz, then take Hoftstallgasse past the Festspielhaus to Herbert-von-Karajan-Platz.

Here, under the sheer cliffs of the Mönchsberg, is an elaborate baroque horse trough, the Pferdschwemme.

Turn into pedestrianized Getreidegasse, Salzburg's main shopping street, with its wrought-iron shop signs. At the end is Mozarts Gerburtshaus (➤ 140–141).

Distance 3km (2 miles)
Time 4 hours without visits to museums
Start point Mirabell Gardens
End point Getreidegasse
Lunch K+K am Waagplatz (€€) ✉ Waagplatz 2 ☎ 0662 842156

More to see in Central Austria

BAD ISCHL

This handsome spa town became fashionable in the 19th century after Emperor Franz-Josef built a summer residence, the **Kaiservilla,** here in 1856. You can still recapture some of the town's faded imperial grandeur by strolling along the tree-shaded esplanade in the direction of the old pump room, known as the Trinkhalle. It was here that Franz-Josef signed the fateful declaration of war against Serbia in July 1914. The Emperor's wife, Elizabeth (Sisi), had her own palace in the beautifully landscaped Kaiserpark, now a museum of photography.

Franz-Josef was a regular at Zauner's pastry shop, birthplace of the delicious chocolate confection known as Zaunerstollen. Another famous café, Zammer's, was popular with Brahms and Johann Strauss the Younger. Franz Léhar, who wrote the music to the operetta *The Merry Widow*, was so fond of Bad Ischl that he built a villa for himself on the banks of the Traun (now a museum).

🚋 5E ✉ 90km (56 miles) southeast of Salzburg 🚆 Bad Ischl

ℹ Bahnhofstrasse 6 ☎ 06132 277570

❓ Jul–Aug operetta festival ☎ 06132 23839; www.leharfestival.at

Kaiservilla

☎ 06132 23241 🕐 Guided tour hourly (at least) Jan–Mar Wed only 10–4; Apr daily 10–4; May–Oct daily 9:30–4:45

✋ Moderate

BRAUNAU AM INN

Shunned by many as the birthplace of Adolf Hitler, Braunau deserves a better press. Surrounded by rolling countryside ideal for cycling, the picturesque little town lies just across from the German border. The 100m-high (328ft) tower of the Gothic Stefanskirche is a local landmark. Part of the town's medieval walls also survive, notably the Torturm (Gate Tower) with its miniature carillon. The main square is lined with pastel-coloured burghers' houses dating from the 16th and 17th centuries.

🚋 3C ✉ 45km (28 miles) north of Salzburg 🚆 Braunau am Inn

ℹ Stadtplatz 2 ☎ 07722 62644

EISRIESENWELT

Best places to see, ➤ 38–39.

FREISTADT

This delightful little town lies in the Mühlviertel, a region once famous for its mills. In medieval times Freistadt was an important border post on the salt route to Bohemia. Nowadays its remarkably preserved fortifications, dating from the 14th and 15th centuries, are a major tourist attraction. It will take you about half an hour to complete a circuit of the towers, gateways and double walls. Next, head for the Hauptplatz, the resplendent central square with pastel coloured baroque houses. On one side is the late-Gothic Schloss, now home to the **Heimatmuseum (District Museum),** which contains an unusual collection of painted glass. Of more general interest is the 15th-century Pfarrkirche (St Catherine's Church). It was given a baroque face-lift but the original tower – a local landmark – survives. If you're here for more than a day you might consider driving over to Kefermarkt (11km/ 7 miles) where the Wolfgangskirche has an exquisitely carved altarpiece dating from 1497. More than 40m (130ft) high, it's rated as one of the finest in Europe.

✚ 7C ✉ 120km (75 miles) northeast of Salzburg 🚉 Freistadt (3km/ 2 miles)

🛈 Hauptplatz 14 ☎ 07942 75700

Heimatmuseum Schlossholz

☎ 07942 72274 🕐 Mon–Fri 9–12, 2–5, Sat 2–5

GMUNDEN

This popular Salzkammergut resort has a lovely riverine setting at the northern tip of the Traunsee. Once the haunt of emperors – Kaiser Wilhelm II of Germany and Nicholas II of Russia to name but two – Gmunden continues to exude affluence and contentment. The focal point is the esplanade which runs along the lakefront towards the beach and harbour, where you can waterski and windsurf as well as sail. There are lake cruises on a 19th-century paddle-steamer, *Gisela*, which once carried the Emperor Franz-Josef; alternatively you could take a look at the 17th-century

Landschloss before strolling across the wooden bridge to Schloss Ort, the 'castle-on-the-lake'.

Schloss Ort dates from the 15th century, but was acquired in 1878 by an obscure Habsburg, Archduke Salvator, who used the alias of Johann Ort before disappearing in South America. For stunning views take the **cable-car** to the top of the Grünberg (833m/2,733ft).

✚ 5D 🚉 Gmunden 🚢 *Gisela*, Traunseeschiffahrt Eder ☎ 07612 66700
🛈 Am Graben 2 ☎ 07612 64305

Cable-car
✉ Freygasse 4 🕐 May–Oct daily 9–5; Jul–Aug daily 9–6 💵 Expensive

GURKTAL

The Gurk valley is a charming region of lakes, hilltop castles and historic old towns like Villach, with its picturesque medieval centre, ruined Schloss and boat trips on the River Drau. Just to the north is the tranquil Ossiacher See and the holiday resort of Ossiach – home of the Carinthian Summer Music Festival. The main appeal of St Veit an der Glan lies in its Renaissance and baroque architecture, notably the splendid Rathaus (Town Hall), with its arcaded courtyard and state rooms, open for guided tours. No one travelling through the Gurktal should miss **Schloss Hochosterwitz,** the last word in fairy-tale castles and the inspiration for Walt Disney's film *Snow White*. The 14 defensive gates were designed to withstand attacks from the Turks. You'll find more splendid military architecture in Friesach, an old fortress town with a medieval keep and walls partly intact. The main attraction in Gurk itself is the magnificent 12th-century Romanesque cathedral. For something different, visit the Zwergenpark with its comic garden statues and miniature railway.

✚ 19K ✉ 25km (15.5 miles) north of Klagenfurt 🚉 Villach, St Veit
🛈 Dr Schnerichstrasse 12, Gurk ☎ 04266 8125

Schloss Hochosterwitz

☎ 04213 2020/2507 🕗 Apr–Oct daily 9–5; May–Sep daily 8–6 ✋ Moderate

HALLSTATT

Best places to see, ➤ 40–41.

KLAGENFURT

This historic old town came into its own in 1518 when Maximilian I designated it the capital of Kärnten (Carinthia). Its beautifully preserved inner core, much of it pedestrianized, has won several

awards and is worth at least half a day's exploration. Though not as lively as some resorts on the Wörther See, Klagenfurt is a convenient base for exploring the lake and the surrounding countryside and has attractions specially suited to children.

The most impressive sights are the town houses with their arcaded courtyards. Neuer Platz is the focal point, with its exceptional 16th-century Dragon Fountain (the dragon is the town's emblem). In the Alter Platz, behind the Plague Column (1680) and House of the Golden Goose (1489), is the twin-towered Landhaus (1590), former seat of the provincial assembly. Climb one of the arcaded staircases to the Wappensaal (Ceremonial Hall), emblazoned with the coats of arms of the Carinthian nobility. The cathedral (Domkirche) was built by Protestants but handed over to the Jesuits who reconsecrated it in 1604.

To reach Wörther See (3km/2 miles from town) take Villacherstrasse. On the way, you'll pass the popular Minimundus theme park (➤ 60). Boat cruises explore the scenic Lendkanal, while trips on the lake leave from near the Strandbad (beach).

✚ 20K ◨ Klagenfurt ⛴ Lendkanal: mid-May to mid-Sep, further details from tourist office; Wörther See: Wörthersee Schiffahrt ☎ 0463 21155
✈ Internal flights
ℹ Rathaus, Neuer Platz 1 ☎ 0463 5372223/2293

a drive in the Upper Mur Valley

Leave Klagenfurt on Bundestrasse 83, passing through the pretty medieval town of St Veit an der Glan on the way to Friesach.

The oldest town in Carinthia, Friesach has retained much of its medieval fortifications, including a water-filled moat.

Continue on route 83 to Neumarkt, and turn left to St Lambrecht (on the Lassnitz road).

The imposing 14th-century monastery of St Lambrecht (look for the twin-towered church) is worth a short stop. The major attraction is the baroque Stiftskirche (abbey church), while the Gothic-style Peterskirche across the courtyard makes a pleasing contrast.

Continue on the side road to Murau.

There's enough here to keep you busy for an hour or two and, if it's not your turn at the wheel, enjoy a glass of the local Murauer beer. Murau has been producing beer for more than 500 years and the Brauhaus (brewery) has a restaurant, souvenir shop and museum. If you're feeling energetic, climb the hill to the 17th-century Schloss Obermurau (closed to the public) and the 13th-century parish church with a fresco of St Anthony and his pig.

From Murau follow the river westwards on Bundestrasse 97. Turn south at Stadl an der Mur, crossing the Gurktaler Alps to the junction with Bundestrasse 93. Turn left to Gurk (➤ 150). Continue on route 93 through Strassburg. At the junction with route 83 turn right to return to Klagenfurt.

Distance 198km (123 miles)
Time 8 hours
Start/end point Klagenfurt
✚ 20K
Lunch Murau Brauhaus (€)
✉ Raffaltplatz 17 ☎ 03532 2437

LINZ

Linz's industrial heritage of steel and chemical plants sits uneasily with a more cultured past, recalled by Mozart's *Linz Symphony*, written on a visit here in 1783. (He stayed at Klostergasse 20, marked by a plaque.) Today it's a lively and interesting place where redevelopment and restoration have gone hand in hand to pleasing effect. Time your visit to coincide with the International Bruckner Festival in September and you'll be in for a musical treat (➤ 25).

If you're not planning on staying long, head straight for the **Landesgalerie** which has an outstanding collection of 20th-century Austrian paintings, including works by Klimt, Kokoschka, Schiele et al. Linz's Hauptplatz (Main Square) in the heart of the attractive Altstadt (Old Town) will stand comparison with any. The main points of interest here are the marble Trinity Column, erected in 1723; the Altes Rathaus (Old Town Hall), where Hitler met a frenzied reception on his 'homecoming' in March 1938; and the Alter Dom (Old Cathedral) erected by the Jesuits in the 1670s. If the weather's kind, there are panoramic views of the city from the **Pöstlingberg,** accessed by **tram.**

✚ 6C ✉ 90km (60 miles) northeast of Salzburg 🚉 Linz (2km/1.2 miles)
ℹ Altes Rathaus, Hauptplatz 1 ☎ 070 7070 1777

Landesgalerie

✉ Museumstrasse 14 ☎ 070 7744 820 🕐 Tue–Fri 9–6, Sat–Sun 10–5
✋ Inexpensive

Pöstlingbergbahn (tram)

✉ Urfahr ☎ 070 3400 7506 🕐 Daily, every 20 mins ✋ Moderate (tickets from Tourist Information)

MARIA WÖRTH AND WÖRTHER SEE

Best places to see, ➤ 48–49.

STEYR

A beautiful market town at the confluence of two rivers, Steyr wears its industrial past lightly. Its wealth stemmed from the iron ore mined in the Eisenerz mountains. Even today, some engines for BMWs are manufactured here. (Anyone interested in industrial history should visit the **Museum Industrielle Arbeitswelt**.) The old town, characterized by pastel-painted baroque façades and gabled, red-tiled roofs, is a gem. One outstanding building deserves special mention: the three-storey Gothic Bummerlhaus, dating from 1497, was originally an inn. The town museum, in a 17th-century granary, has a typical façade with graffiti. Steyr also has proud musical associations: it was here that Schubert composed the *Trout Quintet* in 1819. If you're looking for an excursion, just to the west of town is the village of Christkindl (Christ Child) where there's a post office for sending children's letters to Santa Claus and festive greetings to stamp collectors worldwide. Alternatively, go for a ride on a steam train to Grünberg (17km/10.5 miles) on the **narrow-gauge railway.**

✚ 6D ✉ 30km (16.5 miles) south of Linz 🚆 Steyr

ℹ Rathaus ✉ Stadtplatz 27 ☎ 07252 532290

Museum Industrielle Arbeitswelt

✉ Wehrgrabengasse 7 ☎ 07252 77351 🕐 Mar–Jul, Sep–Dec Tue–Sun 9–5 ✋ Moderate

Steyrtalbahn (narrow-gauge railway)

☎ 07257 7102 🕐 Weekends only Jun–Sep

STIFT ST FLORIAN

Stift St Florian and the surrounding countryside are dominated by a magnificent Augustinian abbey, founded in the 11th century. The monastery's baroque appearance dates from 1686 to 1751, when it was completely rebuilt: the Marmorsaal (Marble Hall) and Eagle Fountain are among the highlights. The ceiling frescoes in the library are by Almonte but also look for works by the medieval master Albrecht Altdorfer, in the gallery, particularly the magnificent Sebastian altarpiece (1518). The Stiftskirche (abbey church) is decorated almost to excess with *trompe l'oeil* frescoes, stucco mouldings and inventive wood carving (the choirstalls are worth a closer look). The church is particularly associated with the 19th-century composer Anton Bruckner. A choirboy here, he was resident organist for more than 10 years and is buried in the crypt.

✚ 6D ✉ Markt St Florian, 15km (9 miles) southeast of Linz ☎ 07224 8902
🕐 Guided tour only (1hour 30 mins) Apr–Oct daily 10, 11, 12, 2, 3, 4
🍴 Restaurant (€€) ✋ Moderate ❓ Summer concerts (Jun–Jul);
www.stiftschor-st-florian.at

HOTELS

BAD ISCHL
Hotel Goldenes Schiff (€€–€€€)
Medium-sized hotel where some of the balconied rooms look
out onto the river. Fish restaurant.
✉ Adalbert-Stiffter-Kai 3 ☎ 06132 24241

GMUNDEN
Goldener Brunnen (€€)
Comfortable rooms in the town centre with en suite facilities.
✉ Traungasse 10 ☎ 07612 644310; www.goldenerbrunnen.at

HALLSTATT
Bräugasthof Hallstatt (€)
See page 78.

KLAGENFURT
Hotel Weidenhof (€€)
A welcoming, family-run business with a great location at the
eastern end of the Wörther See. Sauna, solarium, children's
playground, restaurant. Some rooms have balconies.
✉ Wörthersee-Süduferstrasse 66, Viktring ☎ 0463 281540;
www.weidenhof.at

SALZBURG
Goldener Hirsch (€€€)
See page 79.

Hotel Wolf (€€–€€€)
Friendly, olde-worlde place with characterful rooms in one of the
Old Town's quieter streets. Every room is different, so ask to see
what's on offer before you commit.
✉ Kaigasse 7 ☎ 0662 843453; www.hotelwolf.com

WÖRTHER SEE
Hubertushof (€€–€€€)
See page 79.

Schloss Leonstain (€€)

Surprisingly homey, considering that this hotel is a converted medieval castle. One drawback is the traffic noise; on the other hand the facilities, including tennis, golf and boating, are excellent.

✉ Leonstainerstrasse 1 ☎ 04272 2816; www.leonstain.at

RESTAURANTS

BAD ISCHL

Café Zauner (€€)

Bad Ischl's best known café, Zauner is famous for its desserts – try the *Zaunerstollen* (type of fruitcake).

✉ Pfarrgasse 7 ☎ 06132 23310-20 🕐 Daily 8:30–6

Villa Schratt (€€€)

The former home of Emperor Franz-Josef's mistress, Katharina Schratt, specializes in fish dishes.

✉ Steinbruch 43 ☎ 06132 27647 🕐 Thu–Tue 5–11

FREISTADT

Zum Goldenen Adler (€–€€)

In the hotel of the same name, this restaurant is known for its regional specialities. Try the *Böhmisches Bierfleisch* (beef cooked in beer), made with the local beer, Freistädter.

✉ Salzgasse 1 ☎ 07942 72112

GMUNDEN

Marienbrücke (€–€€)

Trout is the speciality at the Wald Hotel. Eat outdoors in summer, in a wood-panelled parlour in winter.

✉ An der Marienbrücke 5 ☎ 07612 64011

HALLSTATT

Berggasthof Rudolfsturm (€€€)

En route to the salt mines (2 minutes from the cable-car stop), this restaurant serves regional specialities and has a terrace with panoramic views.

✉ Salzberg 1 ☎ 06134 20677

Grüner Anger (€)

Located in a small hotel. Plain but useful, using organic produce.
Dine in the pleasant garden.

✉ Lahn 10 ☎ 0613 48397

KLAGENFURT
Villa Lido (€€)

Stylish café and bistro with a beer garden overlooking the Wörther
See, where you can relax with a *torte* or an ice cream until the
boat comes in.

✉ Am Friedlstrand 1 ☎ 0463 210712

Waldwirt am Kreuzbergl (€€)

This beautiful country inn enjoys an idyllic setting among the
woods of Kreuzbergl. Dine out on the terrace and enjoy the best
that Carinthian home cooking has to offer.

✉ Josefwaldweg 2 ☎ 0463 42642 🕔 Closed Tue

Zum Augustin (€€)

Noisy, crowded beer bar near the Pfarrkirche with plenty of
atmosphere. Carinthian noodle dishes are the speciality of the
house, but you'll need to grab a table early.

✉ Pfarrhofgasse 2 ☎ 0463 513992 🕔 Mon–Sat 11–11

SALZBURG
Bella Vita (€€–€€€)

The full range of Italian cuisine is available in this popular
restaurant a little way from the town centre.

✉ Vogelweiderstrasse 9 ☎ 0662 883338 🕔 Mon–Thu, Sun 11–2, 5–11,
Sat 5–11; closed Fri

Café Tomaselli (€€)

If you only visit one café, it should be this Salzburg institution,
which bursts at the seams with people every day. Enjoy a coffee
and an irresistible piece of gateau from the dessert trolley while
watching the waiters weaving between packed tables.

✉ Alter Markt 10 ☎ 0662 844488 🕔 Daily 7am–9pm, longer during festival

Gasthof Krimpelstätter (€€)

Dine in the atmospheric surroundings of a 16th-century inn, not far from the old town. Standard Austrian cuisine and Augustiner beer on tap. Beer garden.

✉ Müllner Hauptstrasse 31 ☎ 0662 432274 ⏱ Daily 11am–midnight

Stiftskeller St Peter (€€)

The former monastic refectory dates from AD803, and this is thought to be the oldest restaurant in central Europe. (According to local tradition Mephistopheles met Faust here.) Poached fish is one of the specialities.

✉ St Peter Bezirk 1–4 ☎ 0662 841268 ⏱ Daily lunch, dinner

Weisses Kreuz (€)

Excellent Balkan specialities, including spicy fillet steak, courgette (zucchini) soup, and rice with pork and paprika. Those with an appetite can try the Balkan Platter, consisting of five different dishes.

✉ Bierjodlgasse 6 ☎ 0662 845641 ⏱ Closed Tue (except Jul and Aug)

Zum Eulenspiegel (€€€)

Reservations are essential at this restaurant opposite Mozart's birthplace. Ask the English-speaking staff to steer you through the Austrian specialities; also good fish.

✉ Hagenauerplatz 2 ☎ 0662 843180 ⏱ Daily 11:30–10:30

Zum Fidelen Affen (€–€€)

'At the Jolly Monkey' is probably the busiest beer hall in the city, so book ahead to save waiting. Typical Austrian snacks, using fresh ingredients and all well presented.

✉ Priesterhausgasse 8 ☎ 0662 877361 ⏱ Mon–Sat 5pm–midnight

Zum Wilden Mann (€€)

In a secluded yard linking busy Getreidegasse with Hanuschplatz, this small, cosy inn, often overlooked by visitors, serves up inexpensive seasonal specialities.

✉ Getreidegasse 20 ☎ 0662 841787 ⏱ Daily lunch, dinner

STEYR
Bräuhof (€€)
For good local fare and great wines, this welcoming inn in the main square is the place to come.

✉ Stadtplatz 35 ☎ 07252 42000 🕐 Daily 10am–1am

Zu den Drei Rosen (€–€€)
Pleasant restaurant with outdoor dining and very reasonable prices in the Mader Hotel, right in the town centre. The set menu is particularly good value.

✉ Stadtplatz 36 ☎ 07252 53358 🕐 Closed Sun

WÖRTHER SEE
Landskron (€€€€)
Dine out at this 16th-century hilltop castle not far from Villach. Medieval six-course dinners on Tuesday nights (with serving wenches!; minimum of 20 guests, on request).

✉ Burgruine, Landskron ☎ 04242 41563

Schloss Leonstain (€€)
The hotel's stylish Leon restaurant draws on Mediterranean and Thai influences for an unusual, light menu. Well-priced list of Austrian wines.

✉ Leonstainstrasse 1, Pörtschach ☎ 04272 2816 🕐 Closed lunch and Nov–Apr

SHOPPING

CLOTHES SHOPS AND DEPARTMENT STORES
Arkade
Busy shopping mall on a pedestrianized street in the town centre. Shops include Ö Heimatwerk, selling ceramics, fabrics, silverware etc.

✉ Landstrasse, Linz 🕐 Mon–Fri 9:30–6, Sat 9–5

Dschulnigg

The best place to shop for the traditional Austrian folk costume – *Lederhosen, dirndls* etc.

✉ Griesgasse 8, Salzburg ☎ 0662 842376 🕐 Mon–Fri 10–6, Sat 10–5

Stassny Trachtenkinder

Buy your kids traditional Austrian dress – waistcoats, blouses, pinafores, *Lederhosen* and hats, all in children's sizes.

✉ Getreidegasse 30, Salzburg ☎ 0662 842357-30 🕐 Mon–Fri 9:30–6, Sat 9:30–5

Peter Tschebull

Shopping chain selling fashionable ladies and men's fashions and sportswear with a branch in Villach.

✉ Am Korso 23, Velden, Wörther See ☎ 04274 2473

OTHER SHOPS
Christmas and Easter in Salzburg

A bizarre shopping experience with two outlets selling traditional and retro yuletide and Easter decorations year round, The main draw is the thousands of colourfully decorated eggs.

✉ Judengasse 10–13, Salzburg ☎ 0662 841794 🕐 Mon–Sat 9–7, Sun 9–6

Salzburger Heimatwerk

See page 62.

ENTERTAINMENT

CLASSICAL MUSIC AND THEATRE
Hohensalzburg

See page 72.

Marionettentheater

Popular operas and ballets performed by string puppets.

✉ Schwarzstrasse 24, Salzburg ☎ 0662 872406

Mozarteum

Although primarily a research centre, the Mozarteum is also the venue of the Mozart Week festival in January and of other concerts throughout the season.

✉ Schwarzstrasse 26, Salzburg ☎ 0662 88940

Salzburger Festspiele (Salzburg Festival)

The Salzburg Festival takes place every year from the last week in July to the end of August. Concerts include opera, orchestral music and theatre, and there is always a performance of *Jedermann (Everyman)* by Hugo von Hofmannsthal in front of the cathedral. You must book in advance by writing to the address below (also for schedule details). Tickets online at www.salzburgerfestspiele.at

✉ Kartenbüro der Salzburger Festspiele, Postfach 140 A-5020, Salzburg
☎ 0662 8045

Schloss Mirabell

See page 72.

NIGHTLIFE
Augustiner Bräustube

A short, pleasant walk from the town centre (on the slopes of the Mönchberg), this bar is popular with students, locals and tourists alike. The beer is brewed on the premises.

✉ Augustinergasse 4–6, Salzburg ☎ 0662 431246 ⏰ Mon–Fri 3–11, Sat–Sun 2:30–11

Casino Salzburg

See page 70.

Chez Roland

See page 70.

Vis-à-vis

Trendy cavern-like bar overlooking the Salzach.

✉ Rudolfskai 13 C0662 841290, Salzburg ⏰ Sun–Thu 7pm–3am, Fri–Sat 7pm–5am

Western Austria

**The mountainous region
of western Austria
includes the provinces
of Vorarlberg and Tirol
and the western sections
of Salzburger Land.**

Vorarlberg is a region apart, almost cut off from the rest of Austria
by the the Alps and closer both geographically and culturally to
Switzerland. Yet the capital, Bregenz, with the serene Bodensee
on its doorstep, is only 8 hours by train from Vienna and the Alpine
scenery is as stunning here as anywhere in Austria. To most
tourists, the Tirol means winter sports and ski resorts, but it's a
summer destination, too, attracting hikers, climbers, cyclists and
watersports enthusiasts. There's also Austria's highest peak, the
Grossglockner, accessible via the famous mountain highway, and
the gateway to the sublime Hohe Tauern National Park. The capital
of the Tirol is the former imperial city of Innsbruck, an architectural
treasure trove, cradled in winter by snow-capped mountains.

INNSBRUCK

With the stupendous Alpine backdrop of the Nordkette virtually on its doorstep, the capital of the Tirol must rank as one of the world's most beautiful cities. Innsbruck leapt to prominence in the 1490s when Maximilian I designated it the imperial capital.

Nowadays the city is known mainly for mountaineering and skiing, but you can enjoy the delights of the Old Town any time of year. Despite its small size, Innsbruck has a cosmopolitan feel and the nightlife is worth exploring.

➕ 13H

ℹ️ Burggraben 3 ☎ 0512 59850

Domkirche zu St Jakob

Innsbruck's lavish baroque St Jacob's Cathedral was completed in 1724. The interior stucco decoration and ceiling frescoes are by two brothers, Egidius and Cosmas Damien Asam. Hidden among the fancy ornament over the high altar is the church's most famous artistic treasure, Lucas Cranach the Elder's *Madonna and Child* (1537).

✉️ Herzog-Friedrich-Strasse 15 ☎ 0512 583902 🕓 25 Oct–1 May Mon–Fri 7:30–6:30, Sun 8–6:30 ✋ Free, donations welcome

Goldenes Dachl

Completed around 1500, the 'Golden Roof' is Innsbruck's most easily identifiable monument. Maximilian I's palace was intended to symbolize the power of the Habsburgs, which would soon extend beyond Austria and the Netherlands to Spain and the New World. The ornate loggia is covered by a layer of gilded copper tiles which glint and dazzle in the sunlight. Maximilian liked to greet his subjects from the balcony before watching the entertainments staged in his honour below.

The Maximilianum is a small exhibition on the life of the emperor, who, it turns out, was a mountaineer as well as an outstanding warrior and artistic patron.

✉ Herzog-Friedrich-Strasse 15 ⏱ May–Sep daily 10–5; Oct–Apr Tue–Sun 10–5

Hofburg

Rebuilt by Empress Maria Theresa in the 18th century, the Imperial Palace's main attractions are the rococo apartments, although only the Riesensaal (Giant's Hall), with a ceiling fresco by the distinguished court painter Franz-Anton Maulbertsch, is exceptional. Better to focus your attention on Maximilian I's amazing mausoleum in the **Hofkirche** (Court Church) next door. The Renaissance marble tomb is surrounded by 28 larger-than-life bronze statues, representing the emperor's ancestors, real and imagined (England's King Arthur is among them). The figures were designed by Peter Vischer and Albrecht Dürer, a protégé of Maximilian. The Silver Chapel, so called because of the silver Madonna above the altar, contains the tomb of Archduke Ferdinand II.

✉ Rennweg 1 ☎ 0512 587186 ◷ Daily 9–5 ✋ Moderate; children under 6 free

Hofkirche

✉ Universitätsstrasse 2 ☎ 0512 59489-511; www.hofkirche.at
◷ Mon–Sat 9–5, Sun 12:30–5 ✋ Inexpensive

a walk around Innsbruck

The walk begins on Maria-Theresien-Strasse at the Annasäule, a column erected to commemorate Austria's defeat of the Bavarians on St Ann's Day in 1703. To the south you can see another piece of imperial bombast: the Triumphal Arch marked two events of 1765 – the death of Emperor Franz I and the marriage of Archduke Leopold II.

Turn away from the arch and walk up Maria-Theresien-Strasse, Innsbruck's main shopping street. At the end, cross Marktgraben into the pedestrianized Old Town.

Herzog-Friedrich-Strasse is lined with splendid town houses, replete with arcaded façades, oriel windows, wall paintings and carved Renaissance panels. The most eye-catching is the rococo Helblinghaus, festooned with stucco

cherubs, scrolls, leaves and flowers. Opposite is the 14th-century watchtower known as the Stadtturm. Climb to the top for a bird's-eye view of the city.

Follow the road to the left.

Pass the historic Goldener Adler hotel (➤ 78) and continue to the River Inn and the Ottoburg, a corner house dating from 1494 (now a restaurant, ➤ 184).

Return along Herzog-Friedrich Strasse, passing the Goldenes Dachl (➤ 168). Turn left, up Pfarrgasse to the cathedral (➤ 166). Return to Herzog-Friedrich Strasse, this time taking Hofgasse (left). Beyond the arch is Rennweg and the Hofburg complex (➤ 169).

The entrance to the Hofkirche is through the **Tiroler Volkskunstmuseum** (Tirolean Folk Art Museum). Among the colourful domestic bric-à-brac, reconstructed interiors, farming implements, costumes etc, are beautifully carved crib figures from the village of Thaur in the Inn valley (the craftsmen are still at work today).

Distance 1km (0.5 miles)
Time 3 hours with visits
Start point Annäsaule, Maria-Theresien-Strasse
End point Point Hofkirche, Universitätsstrasse
Lunch Stiftskeller (€€) ✉ Stiftgasse 1 ☎ 0512 583490

More to see in Central Austria

ARLBERG

The Arlberg massif marks the watershed between the Danube and the Rhine, dividing the people of the Vorarlberg from their eastern neighbours. Until recently this was an isolated part of the world – cars didn't make an appearance in the remoter spots until the 1940s. Nowadays the Arlberg is a popular, but exclusive, skiing area, patronized by royalty and commoners with matching incomes. Fashionable St Anton is the largest resort in the area. Skiing revolves around the Valluga at 2,809m (9,216ft) but the **cable-car** network also reaches the upper slopes of Galzig, Kapall and other peaks.

In 1978, a 14km (8.5-mile) long road tunnel was built under the desolate Arlberg Pass. The overland route from St Anton winds its way via St Christoph, where a local shepherd built a hospice for travellers in the 14th century. Ten kilometres (6 miles) to the west is Stuben, birthplace of the pioneer alpine skier Hannes Schneider and still a favourite with dedicated skiers. If your thoughts incline more to *après ski*, Lech rivals St Anton as the liveliest resort in the region. The pastoral setting is undeniably appealing and, besides skiing, boating, mountain biking, river rafting and cycling are all catered for, while anglers head for the Spüller or Zürser See.

A few kilometres from Lech is Zürs, the most exclusive resort of all, nestling in the beautiful Flexen Pass at an altitude of 1,700m (5,575ft).

✚ 14L (inset) ✉ 80km (50 miles) west of Innsbruck

ℹ Lech ☎ 05583 21610; www.lech-zuers.at

Arlberghaus, St Anton ☎ 05446 22690

Valluga cable-car

☎ 05446 2352 ⚙ End Nov–end Apr daily 8:30–4:15; mid-Jul to mid-Sep 8–5

BREGENZ

The regional capital of the Vorarlberg is an elegant resort in a lovely location overlooking Bodensee. By the lakeside there are swimming pools, a watersport harbour, a marina and the port from where boats leave for excursions on the lake – it's possible to visit Germany and Switzerland on a round trip if you have your passport with

you. Right on the quay is the imposing neoclassical post office; its foundations rest on wooden piles – most of the land in the lower town was reclaimed from the lake. Behind is the Nepomuk-Kapelle (sailor's chapel), Kornplatz with its weekly market, the Landesmuseum (good displays on Roman Bregenz) and the neo-Gothic Herz-Jesu church, with twin towers and striking modern stained glass. The upper town was founded around 1200 by Hugh de Montfort. The obvious landmark here is the Martinsturm, a medieval tower with an enormous onion dome unceremoniously grafted on in 1601.

For an overview of the lake and mountainscape, take the **cable-car** to the top of the Pfänder (1,063m/3,488ft) where it's said you can see 240 alpine peaks. There are several restaurants at the summit, as well as a free zoo and falconry displays.

The Bregenzerwald makes a good excursion – it's here that you're likely to see traditional Vorarlberg farmhouses with their distinctive wood-shingle roofs. Plan your itinerary to include Bezau, Damüls, Schröcken and Schwarzenberg.

➕ 14K (inset) ✉ 130km (80 miles) west of Innsbruck 🚉 Bregenz ❓ Bregenz Festival mid-Jul to mid-Aug ☎ 05574 407400

ℹ Banhofstrasse 14 ☎ 05574 49590

Pfänderbahn (cable-car)

✉ Steinbruchgasse 4 ☎ 05574 421600 🕐 Daily 9–7 every half hour

HOHE TAUERN
Best places to see, ➤ 42–43.

KITZBÜHEL
Best places to see, ➤ 44–45.

ÖTZTAL

The Ötztal is prime glacier-skiing country, with rock climbing, mountaineering and hiking also popular. Sölden, the 'capital' of the Upper Ötztal, is a major package resort offering summer as well as winter skiing and spectacular Alpine views from the nearby peaks of Rotkogel and Galatschkogel. The steep road southwest of Zwieselstein leads to Vent, a tiny village in the shadow of the Wildspitze, the highest peak in the northern Tirol (3,768m/ 12,362ft).

The other major skiing area lies south of Zwieselstein in the Gurgltal. The popular winter-sports centre of Obergurgl, Austria's highest village, has a more rustic flavour than Sölden although the facilities are comparable.

It was in the Ötztaler Alps, right on the border with Italy, that the mummified body of a 5,000-year-old neolithic trader, nicknamed 'Ötzi', was discovered in the early 1990s. At the other end of the Ötztal, the pretty resort of Umhausen is only an hour's walk from the dramatic Stuiben waterfall while Längenfeld's Pestkapelle (plague chapel) rivals the spa as an attraction for visitors. Called the valley of the 'six steps', as it climbs in six plateaux, this is a delight to explore at leisure.

🗺 16L (inset) 🚌 40km (25 miles) southwest of Innsbruck 🚌 Ötztal

ℹ Rettenbach 464, Sölden ☎ 05254 5100

PAZNAUNTAL

The Paznaun is a densely wooded valley close to the Swiss border, best known for the ski resorts of Ischgl and Galtür. Package tourists are Ischgl's major source of income, winter travellers for the most part. In summer it's still relatively quiet, though for how much longer is anyone's guess. The most popular excursion is the cable-car trip to the Idalpe (2,300m/7,546ft), with spectacular walks in the direction of the Swiss resort of Samnaun.

A few kilometres from Ischgl, the smaller resort of Galtür offers climbing opportunities as well as winter sports, including cross-country skiing. The Silvretta Hochalpenstrasse toll road above Galtür is usually open from mid-April to mid-September and makes an exhilarating drive. The route follows the valley of the Trisanna River, passing through the Bielerhöhe pass and the Silvretta lake (Vermunt-Staussee), where boat trips are possible.

✚ 15L (inset) 🚆 100km (62 miles) southwest of Innsbruck

ℹ Ischgl ☎ 05444 52660

UNTERINTAL

Most of the historic little towns in the Inn valley to the east of Innsbruck prospered from copper and silver mining in the 16th century. There's an underground **mining museum** beneath the Tuxer Alps at Schwaz. Rattenberg, just outside Brixlegg, is also famous for mining. Looming over the picturesque streets are the ruins of Maximilian I's old castle. Much better preserved is the Emperor's 'pleasure palace' of **Schloss Geroldseck** in Kufstein (near the German border) and Schloss Tratzberg, between Stans and Jenbach. Jenbach is also the home of the famous **Riedel** glassware factory and shop. A steam-driven cog railway runs towards Seespitz on the tranquil Achensee.

✠ 15H ✉ 60km (37 miles) northeast of Innsbruck
ℹ Unterer Stadtplatz 8, Kufstein ☎ 05372 62207

Silberbergwerk (Silver Mine)

✉ Alte Landstrasse 3A, Schwaz ☎ 05242 723720 🕐 May–Oct daily 9–5; Nov–Apr daily 10–4 💰 Moderate

Schloss Geroldseck

✉ Kufstein ☎ 05372 62207 🕐 Mid-Mar to Oct daily 9–5; Nov to mid-Mar daily 10–4

Riedel Glass

✉ Weissachstrasse 28–34 ☎ 05372 64896

ZELL AM SEE

With breathtaking mountain scenery and an amazing variety of sporting activities, this charming lakeside resort can hardly fail to appeal. Skiing is the main activity in winter – the ski runs below the Schmittenhöhe (in Zell) and Kitzsteinhorn (in nearby Kaprun) are well suited to beginners and intermediate skiers. At high altitude, you get around by ski-lift and cable-car, while regular bus services link the resorts below.

Zell is ideal for snowboarding, tobogganing, ice skating and curling, and glacier skiing is possible in summer from Kaprun. When the landscape undergoes its seasonal transformation, the lake is taken over by sailors and windsurfers, while the less energetic amble along to the beach.

There's not much in the town itself, apart from the medieval parish church. Boat trips across the lake to Thumersbach, which has its own beach, leave from the esplanade. For something more invigorating, take the **cable-car** up the Schmittenhöhe mountain for panoramic views of the Glockner and Tauern ranges. From mid-May to October you can travel on the Alpine pass, the Grossglockner Hochalpenstrasse (► 180–181). Another 'must' is the 400m (1,310ft) high Krimml Waterfall – take the **Pinzgaubahn,** a narrow-gauge steam railway which winds its way unhurriedly through the flower-strewn meadows of the Salzach valley.

www.zellamsee-kaprun.com

✚ 16H ✉ 100km (62 miles) east of Innsbruck ▨ Zell am See
⛴ Zell–Thumersbach ❓ Krampusläufe folk festival (Dec)
ℹ Brucker Bundesstrasse 1A ☎ 06542 770

Schmittenhöhe cable car

🕐 Mid-May to mid-Oct daily 8.30–5; otherwise 8:30–4:30

Pinzgauer narrow-gauge train

☎ 06542 93000 🕐 Jul to mid-Sep Sun

a drive on the Grossglockner Hochalpenstrasse

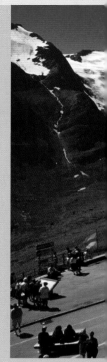

Leave Zell am See (➤ 179) on route 107. At Bruck, the toll gates signal the start of the mountain road.

The road over the Grossglockner pass was built between 1930 and 1935. An amazing feat of engineering, it's 48km (30 miles) long with 39 hairpin bends between Ferleiten and Fuscher Törl – a climb with a maximum gradient of 12 per cent. There are numerous parking areas along the way, all with views, and there's an observation tower at Edelweiss Spitze. At the highest point, Hochtor (2,505m/8,218ft), the road enters a short tunnel and there are more stunning vistas as you emerge.

Beyond the tunnel take the twisting side turn known as the Gletscherstrasse, to Franz-Josefs Höhe.

There's a hotel with a restaurant and viewing terrace. A cable-car takes visitors down to the breathtaking Pasterze Glacier – flowing more than 10km (6 miles), it's one of the most impressive in Europe.

Continue on route 107 down the south side of the mountain to Heiligenblut.

Nestling in the folds of the Hohe Tauern mountains, Heiligenblut (its name means Holy Blood) is especially photogenic when the sun alights on the slender Gothic spire of the parish church. Take a look inside at the

magnificent altarpiece. Almost 11m (36ft) high, it was carved by Wolfgang Asslinger in 1520.

Follow the River Möll to Winklern. From here, the road climbs the Iselsberg Pass (1,204m/3,950ft), before descending towards Lienz, offering fine views of the Lienz Dolomites and the town itself.

Distance 86km (53 miles). Road open May–early Nov, 5am–10pm
Time 9 hours (3 hours without stops)
Start point Zell am See ✚ 16H
End point Lienz ✚ 16J
Lunch Glocknerhof (€€) ✉ Hof 6–7, Heiligenblut ☎ 04824 2244

ZILLERTAL

Apart from skiing and other winter sports, The Ziller valley offers hiking, kayaking, paragliding, rafting and rock climbing, not to mention the scenery which, south of Mayrhofen, is spectacular. The main centre is the Tirolean market town of Zell am Ziller, where traditional rural customs are vigorously observed, typically in early May when thousands of visitors converge to witness the Gauderfest, a lively rural event with folk music and dancing lubricated with locally brewed beer. Ten kilometres (6 miles) south of Zell is **Mayrhofen,** popular with hikers. Mayrhofen is also the terminus of the Zillertalbahn, a narrow-gauge railway which operates some steam services along the Ziller valley to Jenbach.

Beyond Mayrhofen, a scenic mountain road connects the old Tirolean villages of the Tuxer valley, a summer glacier skiing region, very busy at the height of the season.

✛ 15H ⊠ 40km (25 miles) southeast of Innsbruck

Mayrhofen
🚋 Zillertalbahn ☎ 05244 6060 🕓 Jun to mid-Dec (three times daily)
ℹ Europahaus ☎ 05285 6760

ZUGSPITZE

One of Austria's 'must do' experiences is the ascent to this majestic peak (2,962m/9,718ft) on the frontier between the Austrian and Bavarian Alps. The **Zugspitzbahn cable-car** (mid-May to Oct, Dec to mid-Apr) leaves Obermoos (4.5km/3 miles from the ski resort of Ehrwald) for the viewing platform at Zugspitzkamm. From here you can look out over the pine forests of the Loisach valley and the Lechtal Alps. To reach the summit you'll need your passport as this is German territory. On a clear day you can see the Grossglockner glacier, the Stubai and Ziller Alps and, to the north, the Bavarian lowlands.

✛ 16K (inset) ⊠ 40km (25 miles) northwest of Innsbruck 🚋 Ehrwald (1km/0.5 miles) ℹ Kirchplatz 1, Ehrwald ☎ 05673 2395

HOTELS

ARLBERG
Gasthof Post (€€€)
The excellent restaurant is the main draw at this charming, chalet-style hotel. Indoor pool and sauna. The hotel doesn't accept credit cards.
✉ Dorf-11, Lech ☎ 05583 22060; www.postlech.com ◷ Closed mid-Apr to Jun, mid-Sep to Nov

BREGENZ
Hotel Bodensee (€€)
All rooms in this medium-priced hotel have TV and en suite facilities. The breakfast is good value.
✉ Kornmarktstrasse 22 ☎ 05574 42300; www.hotel-bodensee.at

INNSBRUCK
Goldener Adler (€€)
See page 78.

Hotel-Gasthof Bierwirt (€€€)
See page 78.

Hotel Royal (€€)
Don't be put off by the uninspired exterior; the rooms in this conveniently situated hotel are large and comfortable.
✉ Innrain 16 ☎ 0512 586385; www.royal-hotel.at

KITZBÜHEL
Gasthof Eggerwirt (€)
This traditional guesthouse, over 300 years old, has well-equipped rooms and a good restaurant.
✉ Gänsbachgasse 12 ☎ 05356 62455; www.eggerwirt-kitzbuehel.at

Sporthotel Reisch (€€)
Centrally located hotel with oak-decorated interiors.
✉ Franz Reisch Strasse 3 ☎ 05356 63366; www.sporthotelreisch.at
◷ Closed Apr to mid-May, mid-Oct to Nov

ZELL AM SEE

Pension Hubertus (€)

Family-run, eco-friendly guesthouse near the cable-car station, which serves local organic food at breakfast.

✉ Gartenstrasse 4 ☎ 06542 72427; www.hubertus-pension.at

ZILLERTAL

Kramerwirt (€€)

The rooms at this 17th-century hotel are comfortable and there's a sauna as well as a restaurant and bar. No credit cards.

✉ Am Marienbrunnen 346, Mayrhofen ☎ 05285 6700; www.kramerwirt.at
🕐 Closed part Dec

RESTAURANTS

ARLBERG

Krone (€€€)

Trendy hotel-restaurant for gourmets who enjoy game and fish specialities. Attractive location. No credit cards.

✉ Haus 13 (between the river and the church), Lech ☎ 05583 2551

Schäfle (€€€)

Expensive, but this traditional restaurant has a *gemütlich* (genial) ambience and good regional dishes with interesting sauces.

✉ Naflastrasse 3, Feldkirch ☎ 05522 72203 🕐 Closed Sat–Sun

BREGENZ

Goldener Hirschen (€)

Old town inn, with convivial atmosphere. Go for the pasta dishes.

✉ Kirchstrasse 8 ☎ 05574 42815 🕐 Closed Tue

INNSBRUCK

Ottoburg (€€)

Busy restaurant in a late 15th-century house near the River Inn. Upstairs is more exclusive but the choice of Austrian dishes is a little less predictable than downstairs.

✉ Herzog-Friedrich-Strasse 1 ☎ 0512 584338 🕐 Closed Mon

Seegrube (€€€)

Travel by funicular, then cable-car, to dine at 1,400m (4,590ft) on the Nordkette with Innsbruck spread out at your feet and the central Alps all around – breathtaking!

✉ Nordkette ☎ 0512293375 🕓 Cable-car at half-hourly intervals until 11:30pm. Fri only

Stiftskeller (€€)

Located in a quaint alleyway near the Hofburg, this popular restaurant serves a variety of Austrian and fish dishes.

✉ Stiftgasse 1 ☎ 0512 570706

KITZBÜHEL

Chizzo (€)

Good value Tirolean food served in pleasant surroundings.

✉ Josef-Herold-Strasse 2 ☎ 05356 62475

Tennerhof (€€€)

Exclusive (and very expensive) Tirolean restaurant famous throughout the region for the standard of its cooking. Jacket and tie essential and you'll need to book a table.

✉ Griesenauweg 26 ☎ 053566 3181

KUFSTEIN

Hotel Zum Bären (€€€)

Excellent restaurant in a 17th-century hotel. The cuisine focuses on Tirolean specialities.

✉ Salurnerstrasse 36 ☎ 05372 62229

ZELL AM SEE

Café Feinschmeck (€€)

Welcoming café-restaurant in hotel in the pedestrianized town centre. Austrian standards including turkey *Schnitzel* (cutlet fried in breadcrumbs) and there's a non-smoking section.

✉ Dreifaltigkeitsgasse 10 ☎ 06542 72549

Schloss Prielau (€€€)
A castle setting for this grand and elegant restaurant presenting mainstream Austrian cuisine with flair and imagination.
✉ Hofmannsthalstrasse 12 ☎ 06542 729110

ZILLERTAL
Gerloserhof (€)
For skiers and hikers; portions are generous and well prepared.
✉ Gerlos ☎ 05284 5244

Kramerwirt (€€€)
Excellent venue for quality Tirolean cuisine. No credit cards.
✉ Am Marienbrunnen 346, Mayrhofen ☎ 05285 6700

SHOPPING

Geigenbaumeister
The shop sells violin accessories but the real draw is local craftsman Wolfgang Kozák. You can watch him repairing old musical instruments and making new ones.
✉ Universitätsstrasse 3–1, Innsbruck ☎ 0512 573402

Sportler Witting
A wide range of sports clothes and equipment.
✉ Maria-Theresien-Strasse 39, Innsbruck ☎ 0512 589144

Swarovski
See page 62.

ENTERTAINMENT

Couch Club
See page 70.

Tiroler Landestheater
See page 72.

Filou
See page 70.

Sight Locator Index

This index relates to the maps on the covers. We have given map references to the main sights of interest in the book. Grid references in italics indicate sights featured on the town plans. Some sights within towns may not be plotted on the maps.

Index

Acknowledgements

The Automobile Association would like to thank the following photographers and companies for their assistance in the preparation of this book.

Abbreviations for the picture credits are as follows – (t) top; (b) bottom; (c) centre; (l) left; (r) right; (AA) AA World Travel Library

4l Heiligenblut, AA/A Baker; **4c** Arlberg massif, AA/M Adelman; **4r** Maria Worth, AA/A Baker; **5l** Hohe Tauern, AA/A Baker; **5c** Austrian National Library, Vienna, AA/M Siebert; **6/7** Heiligenblut, AA/A Baker; **8/9** Innsbruck, AA/P Baker; **10/11t** Near Leogang, AA/P Baker; **10bl** Church detail, Wolfsburg, AA/A Baker; **10br** Stubaital Valley, Tirol, AA/A Baker; **11cl** Hall in Tirol, AA/A Baker; **12bl** Heuriger (wine tavern), AA/D Noble; **12br** Chefs cooking, Vienna, AA/M Siebert; **13tl** Bar, Bermuda Triangle area, Vienna, AA/C Sawyer; **13tr** Naschmarkt (fruit market), Vienna AA/D Noble; **13b** Reinprecht heuriger, Vienna, AA/M Siebert; **14bl** Cafe Schwarzenberg, Vienna, AA/M Siebert; **14bl** Pastries, Vienna, AA; **14/15b** Pastries, Vienna, AA/D Noble; **15r** Cafe Demel, Vienna, AA/M Siebert; **16l** Cafe scene, Vienna, AA; **17t** Mountains near Lavant, AA/A Baker; **16/17b** Waitress, AA/M Siebert; **18t** Karlskirche, Vienna, AA/M Siebert; **18bl** Fountain detail by Vienna's Parliament Building, AA/D Noble; **19tr** St Wolfgang, AA/P Baker; **19bl** Johann Strauss, Stadpark, Vienna, AA/D Noble; **20/21** Arlberg massif, AA/M Adelman; **24** Mayrhofen Festival Parade, AA/P Baker; **26** Tram, Vienna, AA/D Noble; **27** Europa Bridge, AA/A Baker; **28/29** River Danube, Vienna, AA/D Noble; **31** Karlsplatz Station, Vienna, AA/D Noble; **34/35** Maria Worth, AA/A Baker; **36/37** Duernstein Castle, ANTO www.austria.info/Bohnacker; **38/39** Hohenwerfen fortress, ANTO www.austria.info/Weinhaeupl W; **40/41** Hallstatt, AA/D Noble; **42** Hohe Tauern, AA/A Baker; **43** Glacier, Hohe Tauern, AA/A Baker; **44** Kitzbuhel, AA/A Baker; **45** Hahnenkamm mountain, Kitzbuhel, ANTO www.austria.info/Ascher; **46** Kunsthistorisches Museum, AA/D Noble; **47tl** Kunsthistorisches Museum, AA/C Sawyer; **47r** Kunsthistorisches Museum, AA/D Noble; **48/49t** Maria Worth, AA/A Baker; **48b** Worther See at Velden, AA/A Baker; **50** Melk Abbey, ANTO www.austria.info/Trumler; **52/53t** Schloss Schonnbrunn, AA/C Sawyer; **52b** Schloss Schonnbrunn, AA/D Noble; **54/55** Museum of Modern Art, ANTO www.austria.info/Bartl; **56/57** Lake Klopeiner See, ANTO www.austria.info/Bartl; **58/59** View from the Zwolferhorn towards St Gilgen, AA/A Baker; **61** Zell am See, AA/P Baker; **62/63** Souvenir stein. Saltsburg, AA/J Smith; **64** Skiers, Zell Am See, AA/P Baker; **65** View from Zwolferhorn cable car to St Gilgen, AA/A Baker; **66/67** Zeller See, AA/A Baker; **69** Kunsthistorisches Museum, AA/D Noble; **71** Casino, AA/J Wyand; **72** Kursalon, Vienna, AA/J Smith; **74** Graben, Vienna, AA/D Noble; **77** Sachertorte and Apple Strudel, Vienna, AA; **79** Im Palais Schwarzenberg, AA/J Smith; **80/81** Austrian National Library, Vienna, AA/M Siebert; **83** Burgtheater, Vienna, AA/D Noble; **84bl** Vienna, AA/M Siebert; **84/85** Liebenberg Monument and University, Rathausplatz, AA/M Siebert; **85tr** Fountain by Parliament Building, Vienna, AA/D Noble; **85br** Batthany Palais, Vienna, AA/C Sawyer; **86** Neue Hofburg, AA/D Noble; **87tr** Heldenplatz (Heroes' Square), AA/C Sawyer; **87b** Alte Hofburg, AA/D Noble; **88** Clock Museum, AA/C Sawyer; **89t** Clock Museum and Doll and Toy Museum, AA/C Sawyer; **89b** Clock Museum, AA/C Sawyer; **90/91** Peterskirche, AA/D Noble; **91br** Detail on Peterskirche, AA/C Sawyer; **92b** Prater Park, AA/M Siebert; **93t** Ferris Wheel, Prater Park, AA/M Siebert; **94tl** Schloss Belvedere, AA; **94cl** Schloss Belvedere, AA/D Noble; **95t** Cascades, Schloss Belvedere, AA/D Noble; **95b** Schloss Belvedere, AA/D Noble; **96t** Ceiling, Servitenkirche, AA/C Sawyer; **96b** Secession, AA/C Sawyer; **97** Sigmund Freud Museum, AA/M Siebert; **98** Lippizaner ornament, AA/J Smith; **98/99** Stephansdom, AA/C Sawyer; **99br** Stephansdom, AA/D Noble; **101** Heiligenkreuz Abbey, ANTO www.austria.info/Trumler; **109** Burgenland, ANTO www.austria.info/Popp G; **110** Trinity Column, Baden, AA/D Noble; **112** Concert, Esterhazy Palace, ANTO www.austria.info/Markowitsch; **113** Kalvarienberg church, ANTO www.austria.info/Bohnacker; **114** Graz, ANTO www.austria.info/Bohnacker; **115** Clock Tower, Graz, ANTO www.austria.info/Bohnacker; **116** Eggenberg Palace, ANTO www.austria.info/H Wiesenhofer; **117** Graz, ANTO www.austria.info/Bohnacker; **118/119** Landhaus, Graz, ANTO www.austria.info/Wiesenhofer; **120/121** Stein an der Donau, ANTO www.austria.info/Wahrmann; **122t** Mariazell, ANTO www.austria.info/Markowitsch; **122c** Gnadenaltar, Mariazell, ANTO www.austria.info/Gruenert; **124/125** Vineyards, Oggau am Neusiedler See, ANTO www.austria.info/H.Wiesenhofer; **126/127** Windmills, Retz, ANTO www.austria.info/Wahrmann; **128** Altenburg Library, ANTO www.austria.info/Trumler; **135** Cafe Winkler, Salzburg, AA/P Baker; **136** Cathedral, AA/A Baker; **137** Statue of Neptune, AA/A Baker; **139** View over Salzburg, AA/P Baker; **140/141t** Mozarts Geburtshaus, AA/J Smith; **140b** Mozarts Geburtshaus, ANTO www.austria.info/Wiesenhofer; **142/143b** Residenzplatz, AA/P Baker; **143t** Hellbrunn Palace, ANTO www.austria.info/Simoner; **144** Giant chess, AA/P Baker; **145** Mural near Getreidegasse, AA/J Smith; **146** Kaiservilla, AA/A Baker; **147** Kaiservilla, AA/A Baker; **149** Gmunden am Traunsee, ANTO www.austria.info/Weinhaeupl W, **150** Hochosterwitz, AA/A Baker; **151** Dragon fountain, Klagenfurt, AA/A Baker; **152cl** St Veit an der Glan, AA/A Baker; **152/153** Friesach, AA/A Baker; **154** Linz, AA/M Adelman; **155** Linz, AA/Martyn Adelman; **156** Bummerlhaus, Steyr, ANTO www.austria.info/Trumler; **157** Library, Monastery of St Florian, ANTO www.austria.info/Trumler; **165** St Anne's Column, Maria-Theresien-Strasse, Innsbruck, AA/P Baker; **166l** Old Town, Innsbruck, AA/A Baker; **166/167** Innsbruck, AA/P Baker; **168** Old Town, Innsbruck, AA/P Baker; **169** Hofburg, AA/P Baker; **170** Herzog-Friedrich-Strasse, AA/P Baker; **171t** Triumphal Gateway, Maria-Theresien-Strasse, AA/P Baker; **171cr** Detail of St Anne's Column, Maria-Theresien-Strasse, AA/P Baker; **172/173** St Anton am Arlberg, AA/A Baker; **174/175t** Bregenz, AA/M Adelman; **174b** Bregenz, AA/M Adelman; **176/177** Obergurgl, AA/A Baker; **178** Kufstein, AA/A Baker; **179** Schmittenhöhe massif near Zell am See, AA/P Baker; **180/181** Glacier, Grossglockner, AA/A Baker; **182** Mayrhofen, Zillertal, AA/A Baker.

Every effort has been made to trace the copyright holders, and we apologise in advance for any accidental errors. We would be happy to apply the corrections in the following edition of this publication.

Dear Reader

Your comments, opinions and recommendations are very important to us. Please help us to improve our travel guides by taking a few minutes to complete this simple questionnaire.

You do not need a stamp (unless posted outside the UK). If you do not want to cut this page from your guide, then photocopy it or write your answers on a plain sheet of paper.

Send to: **The Editor, AA World Travel Guides,**
FREEPOST SCE 4598, Basingstoke RG21 4GY.

Your recommendations...

We always encourage readers' recommendations for restaurants, nightlife or shopping – if your recommendation is used in the next edition of the guide, we will send you a **FREE AA Guide** of your choice from this series. Please state below the establishment name, location and your reasons for recommending it.

_____

_____

_____

_____

_____

_____

Please send me **AA Guide** _____

About this guide...

Which title did you buy?

AA _____

Where did you buy it? _____

When? m m / y y

Why did you choose this guide? _____

_____

_____

_____

_____

Did this guide meet your expectations?

Exceeded ☐   Met all ☐   Met most ☐   Fell below ☐

Were there any aspects of this guide that you particularly liked? _____

_____

_____

continued on next page...

Is there anything we could have done better? _____

_____

_____

_____

About you...

Name (Mr/Mrs/Ms) _____

Address _____

_____

_____ Postcode _____

Daytime tel nos _____

Email _____

Please only give us your mobile phone number or email if you wish to hear from us about other products and services from the AA and partners by text or mms, or email.

Which age group are you in?
Under 25 ☐   25–34 ☐   35–44 ☐   45–54 ☐   55–64 ☐   65+ ☐

How many trips do you make a year?
Less than one ☐   One ☐   Two ☐   Three or more ☐

Are you an AA member? Yes ☐   No ☐

About your trip...

When did you book? m m / y y   When did you travel? m m / y y

How long did you stay? _____

Was it for business or leisure? _____

Did you buy any other travel guides for your trip? _____

If yes, which ones? _____

_____

_____

Thank you for taking the time to complete this questionnaire. Please send it to us as soon as possible, and remember, you do not need a stamp (*unless posted outside the UK*).

AA Travel Insurance call 0800 072 4168 or visit www.theAA.com

---